Advance Pra

How Green is

How Green is Your City? has the most rigorous methodology going to separate the bright greens from the pale greens, yellows and reds. Green cities are the future, read this book!

— Randy Hayes, Founder, Rainforest Action Network, Former Director of Sustainability, City of Oakland, CA

With global warming and rising energy prices breathing down our collective necks, it's refreshing to see that cities are providing more renewable energy, encouraging local food production, undertaking climate protection campaigns, promoting alternative fuels and public transportation, creating a better quality of life and working for greater overall sustainable economic development. *How Green is Your City?* provides the first benchmark quantifying and qualifying management innovation and the performance of American cities as they seek to define what sustainability is.

— Hunter Lovins, Co-author, *Natural Capitalism*, Founder, Natural Capitalism, Inc., and Co-founder, Rocky Mountain Institute

Sustainability is more than an environmental issue. It's about our economic and personal security, as well as the health and well-being of our families and neighbors. *How Green is My City?* is a powerful indicator of how prepared cities are to address both the challenges and opportunities ahead. It is destined to play a critical role in leading local governments to help their economies and communities survive and thrive in uncertain times.

— Joel Makower, Founder, GreenBiz.com, and Co-founder and Principal, Clean Edge, Inc.

How Green is Your City? is the first national ranking of 50 US cities evaluating how well cities are doing in implementing sustainable practices based on a comprehensive set of indicators, ranging from air quality to use of renewable energy. This is a must read for city officials and citizens who are interested in how cities are responding to the integrated global challenges of environmental and economic sustainability.

— Prof. Susan M. Wachter, Co-director, Institute for Urban Research, and Director, Wharton GeoSpatial Initiative, The Wharton School, University of Pennsylvania

Cities provide the home for the majority of the earth's population and are the greatest consumers of energy, water and resources; they also are tremendous generators of waste and pollution. Billions of city dwellers can be unwitting armies of mass destruction or powerful forces for planetary healing, depending on their city's environmental and sustainability performance. *How Green is Your City?* provides timely and vital information and feedback to city residents and policy makers to help them more rapidly shift their public systems and private lifestyles toward repair and revitalization.

— Andy Lipkis, Founder and President, TreePeople

San Francisco is honored to be awarded by SustainLane in its comprehensive sustainability City Rankings study. Sustainability is important not only for protecting citizens' health and ensuring a great quality of life here in San Francisco, but also for boosting the local economy with jobs and services in everything from clean technologies to fresh food and green building products produced in California.

— Gavin Newsom, Mayor, San Francisco

As America's largest city, New York is honored to be recognized by SustainLane as one of the country's ten most sustainable cities. Putting principles of sustainable development into practice is crucial to making sure that this city continues to be a place where people want to live and businesses want to grow in the 21st century. We know that our city must lead by example and we are working hard to make the 'Big Apple' a green apple.

— Michael R. Boomberg, Mayor, New York City

Surveys such as SustainLane's go a long way toward helping the nation understand what constitutes a better and more sustainable urban environment.

— *The Washington Post*, June, 2006

How Green is Your City?

Dear Peggy,

The SustainLane US City Rankings

★ ★ ★ ★ ★ ★ ★ ★ ★ ★

How Green IS YOUR City?

Warren Karlenzig with Frank Marquardt,
Paula White, Rachel Yaseen & Richard Young

Thanks for letting me (welcoming me!) into your exciting world. Let's move mountains together.

Best,
Warren Karlenzig

New Society Publishers

Cataloging in Publication Data:
A catalog record for this publication is available from the National Library of Canada.

Cover design by Diane McIntosh.
Cover photos (clockwise, upper right): Austin, Texas skyline; San Francisco Ferry Plaza Farmers' Market; Light rail line in Denver; Chicago City Hall green rooftop; Minneapolis from Mississippi River; LEED Certified Vellum Natural Capital Center in Portland, Oregon; Oakland panorama from Oakland hills; Willamette River in Portland, Oregon; Grand Central Station in New York City; Seattle's Pike Place Market.

Printed in Canada.
First printing February 2007.

Paperback ISBN: 978-0-86571-595-0

Inquiries regarding requests to reprint all or part of *How Green is Your City?* should be addressed to New Society Publishers at the address below.

To order directly from the publishers, please call toll-free (North America) 1-800-567-6772, or order online at www.newsociety.com

Any other inquiries can be directed by mail to:

New Society Publishers
P.O. Box 189, Gabriola Island, BC
V0R 1X0, Canada
1-800-567-6772

New Society Publishers' mission is to publish books that contribute in fundamental ways to building an ecologically sustainable and just society, and to do so with the least possible impact on the environment, in a manner that models this vision. We are committed to doing this not just through education, but through action. We are acting on our commitment to the world's remaining ancient forests by phasing out our paper supply from ancient forests worldwide. This book is one step toward ending global deforestation and climate change. It is printed on acid-free paper that is **100% old growth forest-free** (100% post-consumer recycled), processed chlorine free, and printed with vegetable-based, low-VOC inks. For further information, or to browse our full list of books and purchase securely, visit our website at: www.newsociety.com

NEW SOCIETY PUBLISHERS www.newsociety.com

Contents

Acknowledgments

I want to thank everyone at SustainLane and beyond who helped develop *How Green Is Your City? The SustainLane US City Rankings.*

First, I want to thank SustainLane CEO James Elsen, who suggested a green city ranking back in October 2004 as a way to get citizens as interested in sustainability as they are in their sports teams. The idea came full circle when we presented Portland, Oregon Mayor Tom Potter a trophy for the city's number one ranking during a ceremony set in a downtown sports stadium, as part of the 2006 Portland Rose Festival. James, your support, ideas and interest have been instrumental in this book coming together. (Igor Liner made the original trophy cast in recycled bronze that we awarded to Portland.)

Many other SustainLaners helped along the way: Frank Marquardt and David Hayward for their tireless and good-natured editing; Richard Young, Rachel Yaseen and Paula White for their tenacious researching, city outreach and compelling writing. Aaron Proujansky

also helped develop the research methodology and data management system. Kai-Hua Cheng and Valerie Branaugh helped design and layout the study on our website. Haru Komuro and Nancy Juliber marketed and produced, both on the web and in video. Anthony D'Onofrio, helped develop graphics. Saritha Katikaneni led technical production for SustainLane, and her talented developers put their all into the digital depiction of the study. Ken Ott and Ramsay Millie helped provide production assistance for the final manuscript. Abendigo Reebs was an inspired online marketer in the blogosphere and beyond, as was the Rosen Group in their tireless promotional efforts — thanks Margaret Bensfield.

To Kai-Hua Cheng and Ken Ott for their ability to capture the beauty in the cities around us through the street poetry of urban photography. Also, we appreciate designer Bree Sanchez, who pitched in at a late and crucial moment during production.

Our peer reviewers Sissel Waage, PhD, and Tom Paper, MBA, were rigorous and creative in improving the integrity of the study.

Thanks to the scores of city participants: Randy Hayes and Carol Misseldine bear special mention for their lively brainstorming sessions and support.

Thanks to those who, over the past two years, provided great ideas that were incorporated into the SustainLane US City Rankings.

Cheers to publisher Chris Plant, the good people at New Society Publishers and their inspirational, devoted and professional staff, particularly Ingrid Witvoet, Managing Editor.

And most of all, thanks to my wife, Diana Donlon. Her tolerance of the long hours that produced this work is surpassed only by the helpful editing and creative contributions she made over two years of study and manuscript preparation.

— Warren Karlenzig
San Francisco, December 6, 2006

Foreword

By Paul Hawken

For most of the 19th and 20th century, cities, despite the hardships and suffering experienced in ghettos, were seen as places where culture and intelligence concentrated and evolved. In the latter part of the 20th century, urban decay, environmental problems, and ethnic riots created a rush for the exits and rampant urban sprawl. Cities became more dangerous and inhuman. Post-war modernist planners and architects made matters worse by creating concrete monuments to themselves, hollowing out downtowns into commercial centers that felt like mausoleums at night.

Nevertheless, cities grew exponentially, another negative because of environmental impacts. When Paul Ehrlich published *The Population Bomb* in 1968 he wrote that:

"A cancer is an uncontrolled multiplication of cells; the population explosion is an uncontrolled multiplication of people. Treating only the symptoms of cancer may make the victim more comfortable at first, but eventually he dies — often horribly. . . . We must shift our efforts from treatment of the symptoms to the cutting out of the cancer. The operation will demand many apparently brutal and heartless decisions. The pain may be intense. But the disease is so far advanced that only with radical surgery does the patient have a chance of survival."

Ehrlich predicted England would cease to exist by the end of the 20th century and India would have collapsed while mass starvation swept the globe. It seemed that by the 1970s, no one had anything kind to say about cities. Then, something happened that no one predicted.

Birthrates steadily declined and are still declining. In the developed world, they average 1.6 children per woman. In the developing world, the rate is 3 per woman. In countries such as Japan, authorities even ask women to have more children. Given existing trends, population will peak sometime at or before the middle of the 21st century, and then will begin to draw down for decades, possibly leveling out at two billion late in the next century.

One of the reasons population rates continue to drop is because of cities. A contributing factor to birth control in the world is the urban environment. Population planning is an individual act, but the incentive to plan a family is heavily influenced by urban migration. People are leaving rural areas where children are an asset, and relocating in cities where too many children are a liability. In the country, the emphasis is on work and children provide ready assistance. In the city, the path to a better future rests in having fewer children, who are well educated. Virtually all of the increase in world population that will occur in the next forty or fifty years will occur in urban areas. For example, in 2004 world population increased 76 million: 3 million was in the industrialized world, whereas 73 million was in the developing nations. In that same year, the urban population increased by 64 million.

Two hundred years ago urban population was around 3 percent, one hundred years ago it was 14 percent, and by 1950, close to 30 percent. According to the UN, in 2030, 61 percent of people will live in urban areas and the rural population in 2030 will be smaller than it was in 1995. Every week, over one million people are leaving the country and moving to the city.

Urban migration represents a kind of collective wisdom, and how we configure our cities will be critical to our survival. Regardless of the myths about living close to the land, cities are where human beings have the lowest ecological footprint. It takes less energy, wood, material, and food to provide a good life for a person in a city than in the country. Rather than perceive the city as an ecological sink sucking up the resources of the countryside, which cities can do, cities can also be a kind of ecological ark, places where humanity gathers while we peak in population and develop ecological intelligence for a new civilization. There is wisdom in this that is rather extraordinary. It was not predicted that cities might be the best strategy for our long-term survival and well-being. Yet that is exactly what is happening.

The viability of the urban environments, however, is not a given. Population is still increasing, demand on resources is growing faster than the population, and our climate, oceans, and ecosystems are perilously close to disaster. In other words, while we grow we must use less resources. We must build urban arks that are equipped to navigate the uncertainties and demands of the coming decades; cities have to be redesigned, reimagined, and reconsidered. The sustainable city is a place that interacts with its region and resources in a symbiotic way so as to increase the quality of both environments.

How Green is Your City? The SustainLane US City Rankings is the first systematic report card measuring city quality of life combined with resource impacts. For too long, we believed that more meant better, that energy-, concrete- and automobile-intensive cities would bring us a better life. That tall tale is being replaced by common sense understanding that what makes for a fulfilling urban existence is neighborhoods, farmer's markets, parks, mobility, quiet, greenery, and meaningful livelihoods, all of which require less resources and better design.

Urban sustainability is not an option. It represents prudent governance and provident management by and for the people. A carbon-constrained world is upon us. While international action is required to prevent global climatic catastrophe, cities must lead the way in creating a post carbon environment where people can thrive. What we do in the United States and other developed nations can help far-away cities. Our level of consumption and its attendant wastefulness has set an unfortunate example the world strives to emulate. Now we must set a different example because how people live in India and China will have a direct affect upon our children's futures and vice versa. The upper stratosphere has no national boundaries; nor do jet streams and climate. By creating cities that address the future bravely, brilliantly, and humanely, we create examples and possibility for all cities everywhere.

The worldwide diaspora of immigrants, refugees, and peasants to urban slums is growing. The World Bank has predicted that more than five billion people will be receiving less than $2/day by 2030 in today's dollars. The future of the world is being cultivated in the despair, anger and bleakness in the *chawls* of Mumbai, the *favelas* of Rio, in the *kampungs* of Jakarta, the *shammasas* of Khartoum, in the *pueblos jovenes* in Lima, and in the *umjundolos* of Durban. In Darwinian terms, the slums and squatter cities are a rapid breeding pool for human evolution. Leaders, activists, and scholars will emerge from these places, but so too will demagogues, jihadists, thieves, and mobs. That famous lyric "Freedom is just another word for nothing left to lose" may be true for seekers and monks, but it is not true for the bulk of humanity. Freedom and the rule of law are valued and honored when people have something to lose. Neighborhoods work, and are safe and livable because there is a "we" there. The greening of the world's cities is a profound act of social healing and justice, because sustainability addresses whether people feel hope or despair, are secure or threatened, want to cooperate or compete.

I believe the SustainLane methodology will become international, and none too soon. Providing and analyzing the metrics for sustainability is critical to humanity's future. In the end, there is only one ark, the earth. Cities, like individuals, are passengers on this miracle. All cities must work together in this green and just enterprise to ensure that the journey continues. I believe this book is a critical tool in that pursuit.

Late spring at the Yerba Buena Gardens in San Francisco.

Part I

Introduction

Kai-Hua Cheng

How Green Is Your City?
The SustainLane US City Rankings

Why Green Cities?

The SustainLane US City Rankings of the 50 largest US cities is the nation's most complete report card on urban sustainability. The rankings provide a model of how people's quality of life and city economic and management preparedness are likely to fare in the face of an uncertain future. These indicators gauge, for instance, which cities' public transit, renewable energy, local food and development approaches are more likely to either limit or intensify the negative economic and environmental impacts associated with fossil fuel dependence.

Since the first SustainLane US City Rankings came out in spring 2005, world events have made "sustainability" an even more relevant concept. Hurricane Katrina showed how vulnerable city dwellers can be, and how North America's economy and way of life is largely dependent on often-unpredictable natural and market forces. After Katrina and Rita hit in late summer 2005, destroying New Orleans and Gulf oil processing facilities, gas prices shot up. Prices subsided only to move up again in 2006 to record levels because of global political events combined with the steadily growing demand for oil in Asia.

Neither world politics nor global oil supplies are expected to be stable in the near future. And the carbon emission-created global warming effect on the Atlantic's water temperatures is influencing more stronger-than-average hurricane seasons. So the term "sustainability," officially defined as meeting the needs of the present generation without compromising the quality of life for future generations, has taken on new urgency.

The Stern Report, commissioned by the British government, has confirmed the economic necessity of confronting global climate change at every level possible. The report, written by the former chief economist of the World Bank, Nicholas Stern, forecast that, without appropriate actions, the world will be faced with a minimum five percent annual reduction in economic growth from weather and climate-related events.

Largest 50 US Cities Ranked According to Sustainability Factors

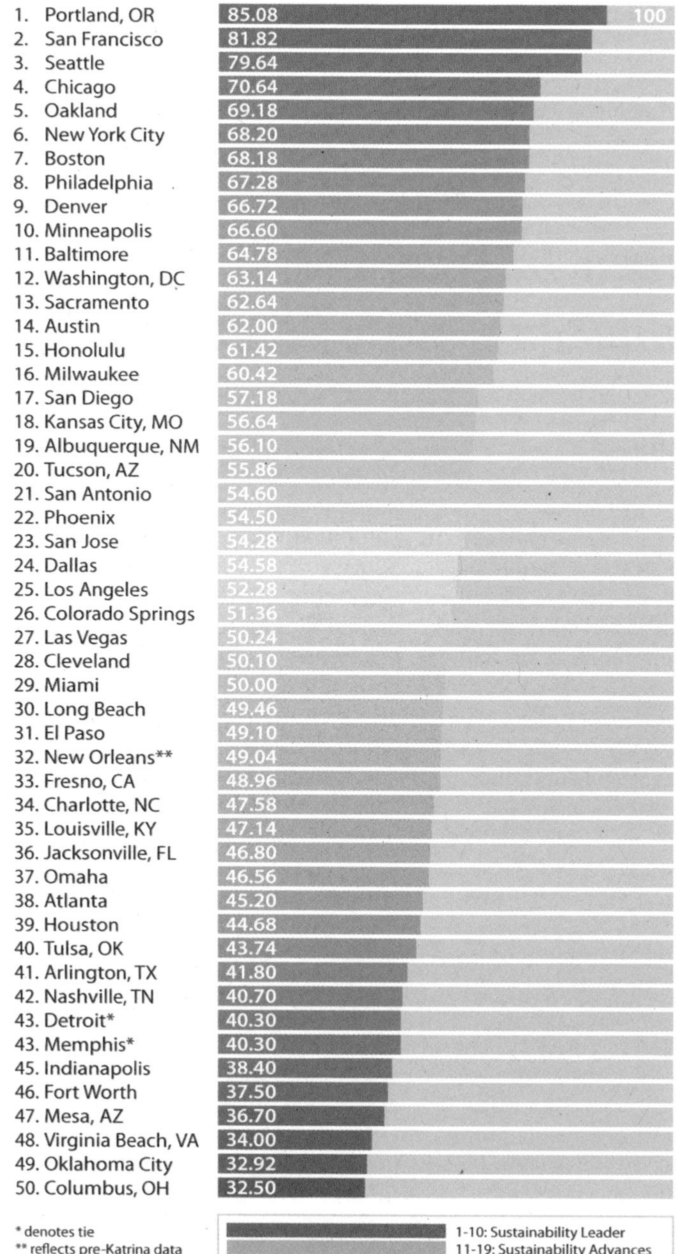

* denotes tie
** reflects pre-Katrina data

Source: *SustainLane*

While global climate change damage is very likely to occur in the Arctic and in developing nations, North American cities are by no means immune. The summer of 2006 saw one of the worst sustained temperature spikes on record in California cities, with more then 140 lives claimed in the state during a single heat wave. At the peak of this 12-day heat wave, temperatures climbed to all-time highs of 119 degrees in Los Angeles County and 115 degrees in Stockton. The state's power grid came close to implementing rolling blackouts, with multiple of days of record energy consumption. Should power failures have been tripped during this statewide event, hundreds, perhaps thousands more, would have died.

No longer can Americans be content that climate-related environmental catastrophes happen to other people. Chicago learned this lesson during a 1995 heat wave that killed anywhere from 485 to more than 700 people; it now prepares for disaster with cooling centers, buddy systems and outreach programs to make sure the elderly and disabled are cared for when high temperature and humidity levels are forecast. In part because of such preparations, the same heat wave that wrought such destruction in California killed far fewer people when it lumbered eastward into Chicago and New York City.

Chicago has become a center of research and project development for these new climactic variations as part of its Urban Heat Island study. Mayor Richard M. Daley and his staff have implemented long-term programs attempting to mitigate future versions of the 1995 heat wave, using green rooftops and renewable energy on municipal buildings as pilot projects. Cities across the country are recognizing the need to change the way they are built and behave to prevent such disasters from reaching the range of devastation wrought by Katrina. To succeed in this effort, a combination of managerial skills, effective policy, economic incentives, technical assistance, and citizen input will be required.

Quality of Life and Clean Technologies

In addition to city energy preparedness and climate change policies, overall rankings for this study took into account quality-of-life indicators such as local food availability, tap water quality, air quality, walkability, park space and roadway congestion.

SustainLane's city rankings also track the growth of clean technologies and other new types of green business. Providing both jobs and tax base expansion, technologies such as renewable energy, transit-oriented development, alternative fuels and green building technologies contribute to a region's economic competitiveness. Now that record venture capital investment and consumer demand are occurring, metro area design and engineering consciousness appear to be scaling up into the mainstream financial realm.

Why Focus on or Rank Cities?

The prosperity of cities and metro areas is critical because for the first time in history they represent the majority of the world's population.

They also consume 75 percent of the world's resources. But unlike most nations or even many states, cities are sited in specific climates with distinct economic qualities and geographic features. Wind turbines, tidal energy and locally produced biofuels capitalize on geographic differences. Local food system development and green building approaches also are the result of regional geographies and climates — food systems and architecture can be further enriched by local cultural knowledge based on the history of a place and its people's experiences adapting to it.

The local nature of every city's economy is reinforced by tax bases, school districts, elections, sporting teams, events, seasons, even the weather. Residents often identify first and foremost with their cities; proximity to other residents and offices of local government mean that many citizens are more directly engaged with their city than their state or nation.

In many cities, you can meet your city's mayor, or at least your elected city officials, without much difficulty or travel. This means that cities get feedback in near real time: when a subway line suddenly needs serious repair or when a water main breaks, city management usually finds out the same day. Said Mayor Greg Nickels of Seattle, which was ranked #3 in SustainLane's city rankings, "I've worked in local government my entire adult life. Because it's a place where you can make a difference: you can roll up your sleeves every day and at the end of the day see the difference you've made."

Nickels first became interested in climate change when a city water district manager explained how the city, which relies on deposits of snow in the Cascades mountains for its year-round water supplies, was increasingly at risk from a steadily decreasing annual snowpack.

That prompted Nickels in early 2005 to mobilize mayors from across the nation to join the non-partisan Mayors Climate Protection Agreement. By November 2006, 330 mayors representing 53 million Americans had signed onto the act, urging the US and state government to meet or beat the carbon reduction goals set by the international Kyoto Protocol, while vowing to take local actions to reduce global climate change.

Because of such powerful urban cultural, economic and political influences, cities are the ideal geo-political medium for sustainability-related improvements, pilot projects and awareness campaigns.

Cities vs. Metro Areas

These rankings focus on specific cities, as opposed to metro areas, as the basis for most comparisons because cities themselves have the ability to directly legislate and manage change. Also, metro areas have a heterogeneous structure that makes meaningful measurement of some factors, such as tap water quality, difficult if not impossible. But more importantly, metro area governance is much more difficult to coordinate, besides being less directly accountable to voter-, citizen- and tax-based initiatives.

Our survey exclusively covered cities in the United States because these presented us with data sets, qualitative measurements and economic systems that could be more easily analyzed and ranked against one another. While some of the greenest cities lie outside the United States — Curitiba, Brazil; Bogotá, Columbia; Vancouver, Canada; and Amsterdam, the Netherlands — statistically comparing cities outside the United States would require a significant additional effort in collecting, analyzing, normalizing and synthesizing data and information.

Since there was no such ranking of US cities when we started in 2004, as researchers we wanted to take on a task that could be informed by similar data sets, weights and measures, languages and geographies. With these resulting data rankings we wanted to provide an impetus for US cities to do better by learning from one another, so that they would then be incented to continually raise the bar.

What Makes a City #1?

The SustainLane US City Rankings focus on the many ways in which city policies and practices differ from one another, and how this affects the people living in those places. The #1 city, Portland, Oregon, captured the top spot with an all-around good to great performance in most every category we analyzed. Ranked below average only in affordability and natural disaster risk, Portland excels in clean technology and green building development, overall quality of life, and in sustainability planning and management.

How did Portland get the top spot? People in the city collectively identify with having a high quality of life more than those in most cities. They work hard at being involved in city policy, boards, projects and practices that impact sustainability. In fact many Portlanders are even able to offer their definition of what "sustainability" means.

Said Portland's Mayor Tom Potter:

> We're definitely proud to be recognized by SustainLane for all the ways Portland's citizens and businesses are working together to create a more sustainable community. In Portland the local governments are leaders for sustainability but it's really the grassroots actions from the neighborhoods and the businesses that make this a special place. The City is buying renewable power and conserving energy, and so are tens of thousands of residents. The City has a green building policy, but it's the builders and developers and buyers who actually change the market. It's the people who shop at the farmers' markets, the growers who manage their farms sustainably, the folks who choose to bike or take the bus to work, and all those day-to-day decisions that are making a huge difference.

One Portland resident and businessperson, real estate agent Kria Lacher, decided to take matters into her own hands in order to make a huge difference. She pushed for the city to adopt a multiple-listing service (MLS) that would list green building features such as energy saving appliances, renewable energy systems, and energy-saving design and materials. After more than 18 months of speaking out at meetings

Green Cities: A Brief History

Large cities, relatively new in the past 200 years with a few exceptions, were advanced considerably with large-scale drinking water, sewage and sanitary systems in the United States during the late 1800s. Meanwhile, public parks and open spaces were implemented from New York City and Chicago to Louisville, Kentucky — thanks to visionaries such as Daniel Burnham and Frederick Laws Olmstead — setting the stage for a grand urban cultural epoch during the first half of the twentieth century.

The end of World War II brought returning veterans looking for affordable housing. In the United States. They were met with government mortgage subsidies offering easy-terms housing loans, and the result was explosive suburban growth. At the outskirts of US cities and in new locations throughout the temperate Sun Belt, a new federal Interstate system, com-bined with a rise in automobile ownership, gave way to a novel way of life called Suburbia. People of all classes, except the lowest classes, could have their private patch of yard, a decent job, and an easy way to get to and fro.

Many older industrial cities, including Chicago, Detroit, St. Louis, Cleveland and Philadelphia, began to experience a steady exodus of inhabitants to the greener suburban pastures, beginning in the 1950s. When jobs began to move overseas and factories began to close, the compounded effect led to decay in the core of once-great population centers. A few US cities continue to lose population at a steady rate.

During the early 1960s, air pollution, once a problem primarily in industrial city centers, was now ubiquitous within urban and suburban areas. Los Angeles, Chicago, Denver, even Portland, Oregon were regularly besieged by brown layers of air pollution known as smog. Around the time the first man walked on the moon, Cleveland's chemically laden Cuyahoga River began to repeatedly catch fire; Americans were made aware, for the first time, that their very atmosphere was at risk.

Reversing the Damage

The administration of President Richard Nixon and Congress took the most comprehensive steps addressing the situation and created in 1970 a new federal oversight body, the Environmental Protection Agency (EPA). Given an agency to enforce what are now called The Clean Water Act of 1972 and the Clean Air Act, cities began to experience cleaner skies and slowly improving lake, river and beach water quality.

But the urban renaissance that was to come in the 1990s was still decades away. Well into the 1980s, blighted areas remained in some cities. ☞

Canopies of neighborhood trees that once covered eastern cities died from disease or old age, and were not replaced.

In 1987 the nation was equally captivated and disgusted by a barge laden with garbage and medical waste that first sailed from New York, then foundered off the Eastern Seaboard and the Gulf Coast. The Garbage Barge, as the nation called it, was turned away repeatedly by port towns that refused to take on its unsavory cargo. Each refusal led to not only greater infamy for the craft, but also a growing realization that landfill space was a finite resource and that, ultimately there is no "away."

The startling discovery of an ozone hole in the earth's atmospheric layer near Antarctica in 1986 preceded the slow realization over the next decade that even more potentially catastrophic global climate change was occurring, fueled by man's rapidly increasing carbon emissions into the atmosphere.

Dawn of the Green City Era

A few cities began to address environmental concerns of their own volition. Austin, Texas implemented one of the first large-scale green building programs, designed to reduce energy and water consumption. A citizen's group in Jacksonville, Florida initiated a quality-of-life indicators program so that progress could be measured and prioritized locally. Seattle began an indicators program using its watershed's salmon populations as the litmus test of the city's ecosystem health.

San Francisco, based partially on the actions of Austin, Jacksonville and Seattle, developed a citizen-led sustainability plan in 1995-1996. The resulting detailed blueprint was adopted in 1997 by the city's Board of Supervisors, forming the basis for a new Environmental Department and providing a way to measure and manage projects ranging from large-scale public solar energy installations to programs for integrated pest management throughout the city's parks.

Throughout the nation, city residents began to do their part on a daily basis by commuting by bicycle, recycling on a significant scale, and making their homes more energy efficient.

Businesses began responding with products and services in green building, water filtration, energy and water efficiency. Based on the rapid reappearance of farmers' markets in cities, residents began to strengthen the economies outside their immediate borders, forming stronger urban-rural linkages first with food producers and, more recently, with agricultural fuel products. These actions began to shorten food miles while making a move toward resource localization. ■

at taking on an entire industry, she succeeded in getting the city to be the first to move to a green MLS for new and existing homes. The change will become effective in 2007, and now other cities are studying Portland's model so they can make a similar change in their city.

Like many who work to green cities, there is precious little opportunity to celebrate victories when so many challenges lie ahead. "I'm just getting started," Lacher said. "The next opportunity is to convince banks to make loans that take into account life-cycle cost savings for homeowners that result directly from these green building features."

Only through scaling up personal networks can cities begin to effectively improve their performance.

Portland has begun using its sustainability ethos as an overall edge to attract businesses, residents, tourists and conventions. Its city slogan, "It's Not Easy Being Green," reflects a marketing savvy that gives the city national currency as one of the capitals of a powerful emerging domestic economic and cultural force.

Other cities are involved in leading the way as well: Chicago in renewable energy and urban greening; Boston, Minneapolis and Oakland in local food development; Denver in citywide transit-oriented development; and Atlanta in green building.

Keep in mind that these overall rankings are based on relativity as measured within different categories among the 50 cities studied and surveyed. Portland is not an entirely sustainable city; nor is Columbus — ranked #50 overall — an entirely *unsustainable* city. Based on the criteria we measured — more than 2,000 data or information points were collected overall — we are confident this ranking reflects which cities are making progress toward sustainability and which ones have a long way to go.

By no means can these rankings be construed as a list of the 50 greenest cities. Again, they are the 50 largest US cities in population ranked according to our criteria categories, then ranked overall by rolling up those separate category rankings into a single overall score.

Of course, there are data that were not included that might have told a more complete story: per capita use of water; per capita use of energy; and per capita production of waste, to name just a few. But since these figures were not readily available in existing data or through the officials to whom we had access, we did not include these potentially important measures. Instead we analyzed what reliable information to which we did have access, such as tap water quality and water importation, renewable energy use, and total solid waste diverted from landfills.

Next Step: Best Practices Knowledge Base

Each of the 50 cities analyzed in this ranking has a dedicated page with a summary of its progress in sustainability programs, practices and performance. Our hope is that residents will learn from this view of their home city, while those in other cities not ranked here have a template that can be applied to their own city's analysis.

If you are an official from any US or Canadian State, province, city or county, please register and submit a best practice in sustainability or environmental management to the SustainLane Government best practices knowledge base: www.sustainlane.us. If you are a citizen, please contact your local government officials to let them know about SustainLane Government's free best-practice knowledge base.

By contributing your community's innovations in sustainability to SustainLane Government's unique knowledge base, your local ideas can be shared and possibly adopted by regional and local government across the world.

Only through scaling up personal networks can cities begin to effectively improve their performance. A learning structure and corresponding open-source information sharing mechanism can more successfully address such critical issues of the day: global climate change, childhood obesity, food and energy security, economic competitiveness and improving the lives of urban dwellers and their planet.

Map of the United States with overlay of top 50 cities by population. Color coded by sustainability progress as of 2006.

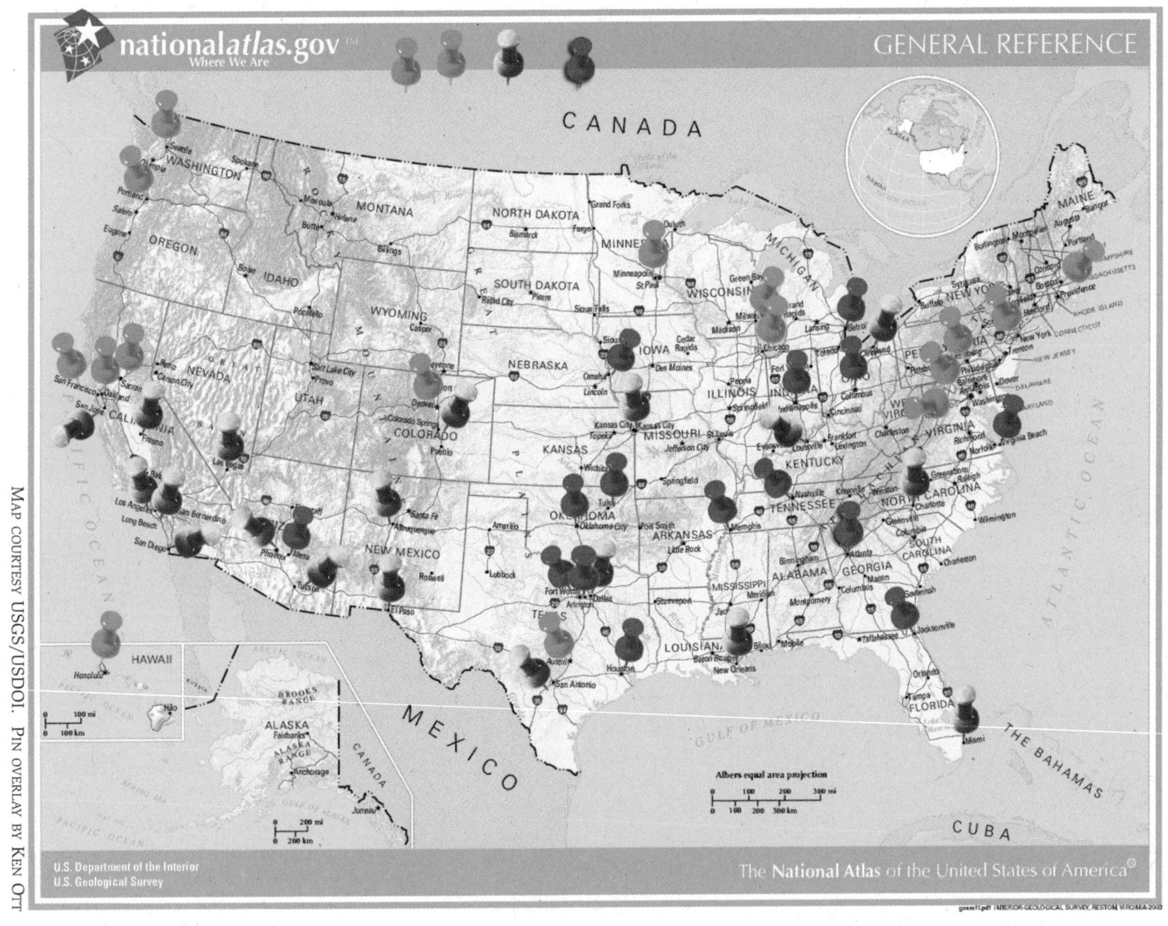

Map courtesy USGS/USDOI. Pin overlay by Ken Ott

How We Did It — The Methodology

Sustainability approaches tend to address combined environmental, economic and social issues, while environmental management approaches have tended to focus on issues like pollution or habitat restoration in isolation. The beginning of the 21st century represents a turning point for cities as sustainability subsumes environmental management practices and policies. Sustainability is a more appropriate approach for urban areas than traditional environmental management because it recognizes that people and institutions are the primary actors that create and benefit from change, with benefits also accruing to natural systems and the economy as a result — particularly in the mitigation of global climate change.

Methodology

How Green is Your City? was developed using a combination of primary and secondary research directed by SustainLane. The 50 largest US cities were included in the study. Data and information on these cities are drawn from surveys and interviews from 2005-2006, and publicly available sources published in the period between 2002-2006.

Overall Rankings

Overall rankings were determined by averaging 15 individual category rankings, each of which was multiplied by a weighting of 0.5, 1, or 1.5 (see "Weighting of Data" for details). The resulting cumulative totals ranged from 85.08 out of 100 for the highest-scoring city (Portland, Oregon) to 32.50 out of 100 for the lowest-scoring city (Columbus, Ohio).

Criteria for Selecting Cities for the Study

The largest 50 US cities by population (based on 2004 US Census data) were selected as the basis for the study. Data and information was collected as it related to the 50 cities proper, with three exceptions. Metro area data collected included regional public transit ridership, roadway congestion and metro area sprawl, as these have a great impact on city air pollution, resource use and transportation efficiency. Air quality data was analyzed on a countywide basis, by which it is collected and reported to the Environmental Protection Agency (EPA).

How Data or Information Categories were Chosen

There are two criteria for how data was selected:

a) *Data or information sets that would be of relatively equal importance to cities across the United States.* For example, water conservation programs were not included because they would be much more important for a desert city in the Southwest than for a city with a plentiful water supply. Cities with exceptional water conservation programs or policies in drier climates were credited, however, under the "City Innovation" category.

b) *Ease of standardized data collection.* Air quality data, for instance, is available in a standardized format freely available (Median Air Quality Index) from the US EPA.

2006 Data Collection and Research Methods

Primary research consisted of email and phone surveys administered to the 50 subject cities during the period between December 2005 and April 2006. Those surveyed included environmental or sustainability departments, energy offices, departments of solid waste, water departments, mayor's offices, and planning departments. Non-governmental organizations (NGOs) working directly with subject cities were also surveyed or interviewed. A total of 37 cities responded to the survey. For the cities that did not respond to the survey, rankings were determined exclusively by data from public and non-governmental data sources.

Data was adjusted on a per capita basis for local food and agriculture (farmers' markets and community gardens), as well as for green (Leadership in Energy and Environmental Design) buildings.

In total, over 100 respondents were surveyed by email or telephone, or interviewed in person. A list of these people and their city or organizational affiliations is included at the end of this methodology.

Weighting of Data

Of the 15 data categories, 11 received a weighting of 1. The remaining four categories were weighted as follows:

Commute to work: 1.5

Weighting was assigned a higher value than all other categories because of the direct and indirect impacts on numerous other categories, including air quality, water quality from surface run-off, greenhouse gas emission contribution to global climate change, road congestion, economic efficiency (expenditures for gasoline leave the local economy; roadway congestion impairs personal and local productivity; air pollution can have numerous health-related economic impacts).

Congestion: 0.5

Weighting was assigned a lower value based on secondary nature of impacts which include reduced fuel efficiency and impaired public transportation efficiency for buses.

Affordability: 0.5

Weighting was assigned a lower value based on secondary impacts — higher housing prices hurt the environment because they force more residents or service workers to commute.

Natural disaster risk: 0.5

Weighting was assigned a lower value because information modeled reflects natural disaster risk only, which depends on climatic probability, insurance information based on past history, etc.

Public Data Sources

Public data from the most current sources were combined in each category to provide ranking metric by issue, listed in italics.

Commute to work

2004 US Census/American Fact Finder commute-to-work information (released in 2004): City resident public transportation ridership percentage, walk to work percentage, bike-to-work percentage; carpool-to-work percentage, drive-alone-to-work percentage.

Regional Transportation

Data from Texas Transportation Institute's 2003 National Mobility Study (Texas A&M) analyzing regional general public transit ridership and square miles per metro area.

Congestion

Data from 2003 Texas Urban Mobility Study analyzing regional freeway and surface road congestion by metro region.

Air quality

US EPA air quality data and information is from fall 2005 (Median Air Quality Index, combined with US EPA Clean Air Act Non-Attainment information, converted to a numerical scale).

NGO and Public Information

NGO and public data sources were combined in each category to provide ranking metric by issue, listed in italics.

Tap water quality

Environmental Working Group's December 2005 US city drinking water database was used.

LEED building

Number of US Green Building Council's Leadership in Energy and Environmental Design (LEED) certified and registered buildings from US Green Building Council, adjusted per capita. A greater weighting was given to data for LEED Certified over LEED Registered buildings, and for LEED Platinum or LEED Gold buildings, over LEED Silver or LEED Certified.

Local food & agriculture

Number of community gardens per city, and number of farmers' markets on a per-capita basis, with additional credit given to those farmers' markets accepting Women, Infants & Children (WIC) federal program vouchers and Food Stamp vouchers. This data came from both NGOs and the US Department of Agriculture, as well as from cities themselves. Cities and/or NGOs provided the number of community gardens per city.

Planning/land use

Urban sprawl data from Smart Growth America's December 2002

study was used. Percent of city land area devoted to parks came from Trust for Public Land (2002 study) and from 2006 SustainLane primary research.

Housing Affordability

Measure of median housing ranking was used, median income was also analyzed as a mitigating affordability factor. Cities with Living Wage ordinances were given extra credit.

Natural disaster risk

Data from Risk Management Solutions' 1999 "Catastrophic Risk in the United States" and SustainLane primary research: cumulative measure of hurricane risk, major flood risk, tornado super outbreaks, earthquake risk and devastating hail risk.

Green economy

Categories credited included whether the city has a clean technology incubator; whether the city or a private organization has a green business directory; and the average number of farmers' markets per capita, and LEED buildings per capita data.

Exclusive Primary Research Categories

Energy

SustainLane primary research analyzed city greenhouse gas reduction tracking; goals and inventories; overall renewable energy use percentage for each city; and alternative fuel fleet data (credit given for cities with 12 percent or more of fleet comprised of alternative fuel-using vehicles).

City innovation

SustainLane primary research analyzed Environmentally Preferable Purchasing programs; commercial and residential green building incentives; carpooling coordination; car sharing programs (public or private); and provided extra credit for other city innovation (general category).

Knowledge base/ communications

SustainLane primary research analyzed whether cities have a sustainability plan; a department to manage environmental/sustainability functions; and research partnerships with federal laboratories and/or nongovernmental organizations. These management functions and collaborations are critical to ensuring long-lasting sustainability program metrics and success.

City and Other Resources for Primary Research

Albuquerque, New Mexico

Martin Chavez, Mayor
Alfredo Santistevan, Environmental Health Department
Mary Lou Leonard, Environmental Health Department
John O'Connell, Environmental Health Department
Deborah Nason, Outreach Specialist

Arlington, Texas

Robert Cluck, Mayor
Robert Ressl, Environmental Services

Baltimore, Maryland

George L. Winfield, Department of Public Works
Stuart Duncan, Department of Public Works

Boston, Massachusetts

Bryan Glascock, Department of the Environment

Charlotte, North Carolina

Pat McCrory, Mayor
Cary Saul, Director, Land Use and Environmental Services

Chicago, Illinois

Sadhu Johnston, Environmental Commissioner
Sarah Beazley, Natural Resources and Water Quality

Colorado Springs, Colorado

William Healy, Department of Planning and Community Development

Dallas, Texas

Karen Rayzer, Director, Environmental Department
Laura Fiffick, Office of Environmental Quality

Denver, Colorado

John Hickenlooper, Mayor
Peter Park, Director of Planning
Beth Conover, Sustainability Director
Lydia Riegle, Mayor's Office

Detroit, Michigan

Vincent Nathan, Environmental Affairs Department

El Paso, Texas

Daphne Richards, County Extension Agent-Horticulture Texas Cooperative Extension

Fresno, California

Terri Saldivar, Public Affairs Office
Christie Kelly, Administration Division
Ken Nerland, Administration Division

Honolulu CDP, Hawaii

Eric Takamura, Director, Environmental Services
Tim Houghton, Department of Environmental Services

Houston, Texas

Karl Pepple, Environmental Programming

Indianapolis, Indiana

Bart Peterson, Mayor
April Sellers, Deputy Chief of Staff
Sarah Besser, Purdue Extension Urban Gardens

Kansas City, Missouri

Kay W. Barnes, Mayor
Bryan Gadow, Office of the City Manager

Las Vegas, Nevada

Tom Perrigo, Department of Planning and Development

Long Beach, California

Beverly O'Neill, Mayor
Suzanne Frick, Director of Planning and Building
Larry Rich, Department of Planning and Building
Kerry Rasmussen, Environmental Services Bureau
John Seevers, Department of Public Works
Chris Garner, Long Beach Gas and Oil
Mike Conway, Department of Community Development

Los Angeles, California

Karin Christie, Environmental Director

Keylaundra McClelland, Environmental Affairs Department

Louisville-Jefferson County, Kentucky

Jerry Abramson, Mayor
Joan Riehm, Deputy Mayor
Cass Harris, Office of the Mayor
Donna Browne, Jefferson County Cooperative Extension
Jason Cissell, Public Information Officer, Metro Parks

Memphis, Tennessee

Jacob Flowers, Midsouth Peace Justice Center

Milwaukee, Wisconsin

Jeffrey Mantes, Department of Public Works
Rhonda Kelsey, Green Team Liaison

Minneapolis, Minnesota

Lori Olson, Environmental Management and Safety

New Orleans, Louisiana

Wynecta Fisher, Environmental Affairs

New York, New York

Michael R. Bloomberg, Mayor
Robert Kulikowski, Environmental Coordination Office
Lys McLaughlin, Former Executive Director, New York Council on the Environment

Oakland, California

Randy Hayes, Former Director, Mayor's Office of Sustainability
Carol Misseldine, Director, Mayor's Office of Sustainability
Scott Wentworth, Mayor's Office of Sustainability
Brooke A. Levin, Mayor's Office of Sustainability
Jonelyn Weed, Mayor's Office of Sustainability
Serena Unger, Univ. of California at Berkeley
Heather Wooten, Univ. of California at Berkeley

Oklahoma City, Oklahoma

Mick Cornett, Mayor
Kim Cooper, Planning
Mike McClure

Philadelphia, Pennsylvania

John Haak, City Planning Commission
David Adler, The Food Trust
Eileen Gallagher, Pennsylvania Horticultural Society
Terry Mushovic, Neighborhood Gardens Association/A Philadelphia Land Trust
Robert Allen, Deputy Managing Director
Leanne T. Krueger-Braneky, Sustainable Business Network of Greater Philadelphia
John Hadalski, Management Services

Phoenix, Arizona

Phil Gordon, Mayor
Karen O'Regan, Environmental Programs
Lucy Bradley, Phoenix Cooperative Extension
Cindy Gentry, Community Food Connections

Portland, Oregon

Tom Potter, Mayor
Matt Emlen, Office of Sustainable Development
Stephanie Swanson, Communications

Sacramento, California

Heather Fargo, Mayor
Sue O'Brien, Chief of Staff
Lezley Buford, Environmental Planning Services

San Antonio, Texas

Dan Cardenas, Environmental Services
David Newman, Environmental Manager

San Diego, California

Linda Pratt, Office of Environmental Protection and Sustainability

San Francisco, California

Gavin Newsom, Mayor
David Assmann, Office of Sustainability

San Jose, California

Michael Foster, Green Building Program
John Stufflebean, Environmental Services Department

Seattle, Washington

Greg Nickels, Mayor
Steve Nicholas, Office of Sustainability and Environment
Mark Brady, Puget Sound Clean Cities Coalition

Tucson, Arizona

Robert Walkup, Mayor
Leslie Liberti, Environmental Services
David Modeer, Tucson Water Director

Tulsa, Oklahoma

Clayton Edwards, Environmental Operations

Washington, DC

Elizabeth Berry, Acting Director, Department of Environment

Other Resources

Scot Case, Former Director of Procurement Strategies, Center for New American Dream
Panama Bartholomy, California Energy Commission
Teresa Parsley, Assistant Secretary, California EPA
Drew Bohan, former Deputy Secretary, Governor's Office, California/California EPA
Dan Burgoyne, State of California
Josh Hart, Former Program Director, San Francisco Bicycle Coalition
Diana Donlon, Independent Consultant, Food Systems
Daniel Imhoff, Author
Eileen Brady, Former VP, Ecotrust
Peter Harnik, Director, Center for Park Excellence, Trust for Public Land

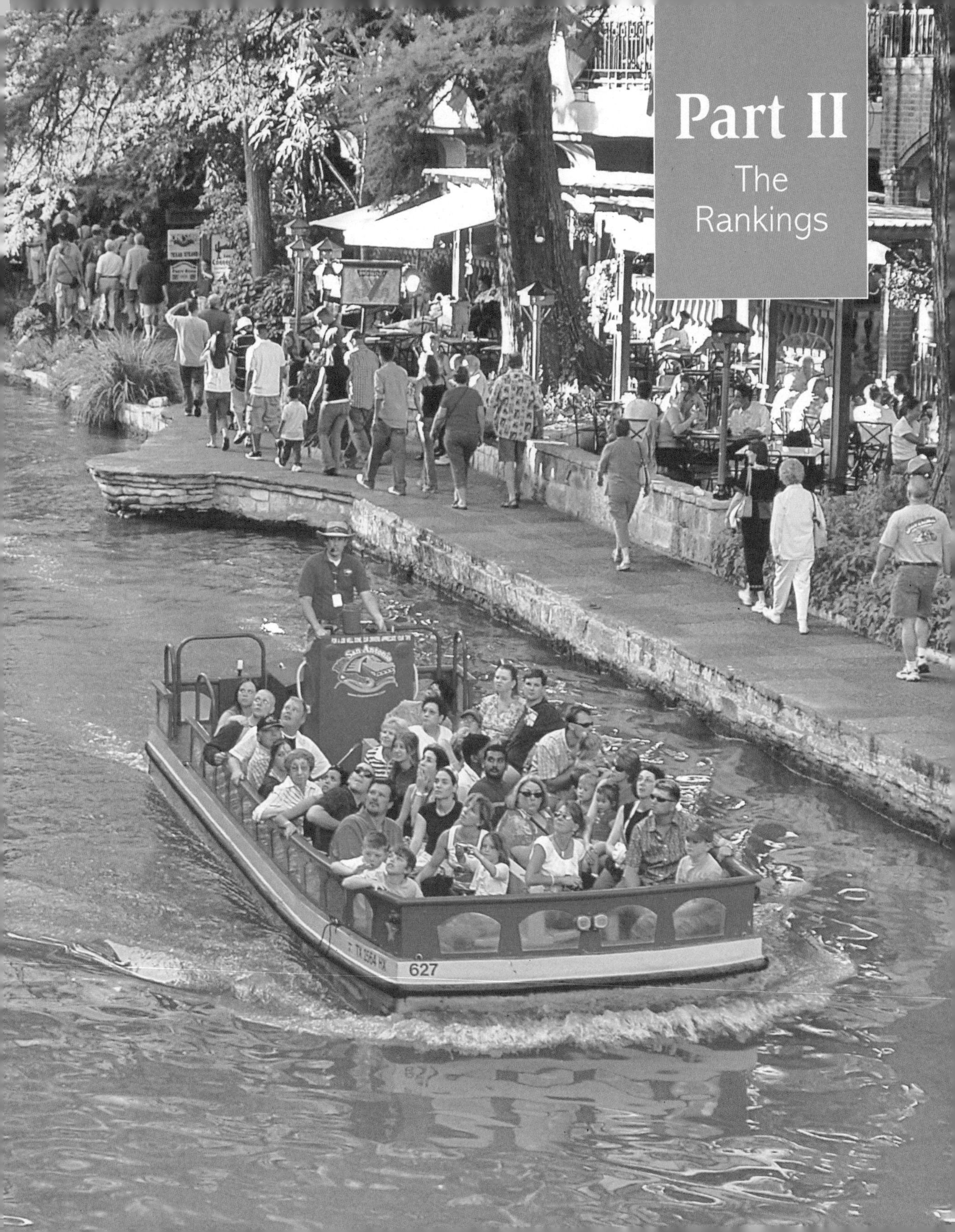

Part II
The Rankings

1

Portland, Oregon

A Role Model for the Nation

Cut out of the forest, Portland offers plenty of parks and bike lanes as well as stunning views of Mt. Hood. Locally owned cafés, restaurants — and markets are integrated into most neighborhoods, encouraging people to walk rather than drive. Air and water quality are among the best in our study. Public transportation, including free transit downtown, is excellent, and mixed-use development in downtown's Pearl District is an urban model for cities across the nation.

In fact, the Portland Visitors Association's official slogan, "It's Not Easy Being Green" reflects Portland's commitment to creating a healthy, sustainable city. It's no wonder other cities look to Portland for leadership and inspiration. In 1993, it was the first US city to attempt to reduce greenhouse gas emissions, and its #1 ranking in city innovation, energy/climate change policy and knowledge base/communications reflects a deep-seated understanding of sustainability management practices. Citizens and politicians have worked together to keep the city's pristine environment in synch with its emerging clean tech economy.

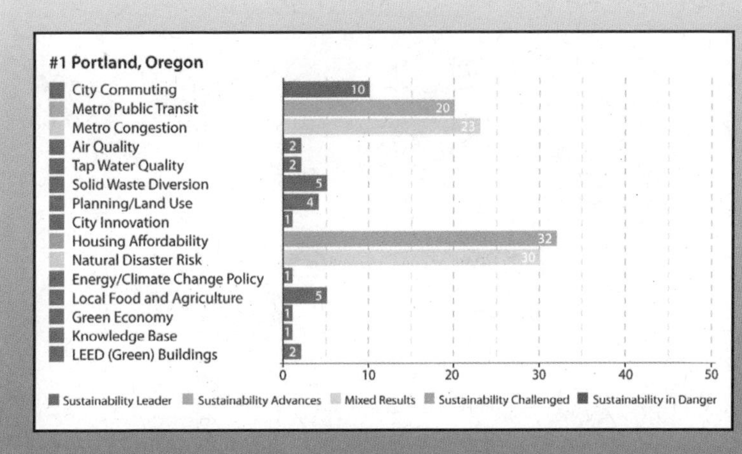

And while Portland residents luck out by having plentiful fresh water from nearby Mt. Hood and clean breezes that blast down the Columbia River Gorge from the Pacific, Portlanders themselves deserve credit for working hard to preserve the natural environment they're blessed with.

A local citizens' movement called City Repair is emblematic of Portland's approach to greening the city. This organization works in local neighborhoods convening people to collectively plan improvements for intersections and other public areas using art, vegetable plantings, information kiosks and bus shelters beautifully built from recycled material.

"It all starts with connecting people and getting them working together," says Katrina Zavalney, who has worked with City Repair since 1999. "Once people start connecting and working together, relationships build and that's when the solution will come. In true permaculture fashion there has to be time to understand the problem and then bring things together to solve the issue."

Free streetcar serving Portland's downtown Pearl District, which is a leading case study for successful urban redevelopment.

Healthy Living

Portland ranks #9 in percent of land devoted to parks, which make up 15 percent of the city's total footprint. You can run, hike or cycle in 5,000-acre Forest Park, one of the nation's largest urban forest areas — sometimes without bumping into another soul. Forest Park and other regional parks also help protect the area's tap water, which rates #2 in the study. The air is relatively clean, too

(ranking #2), with no violations of the Clean Air Act standards in any category.

Portland is also at the forefront of local food movements. The city government formed a food advisory council, and Mayor Tom Potter has urged citizens to buy at least 10 percent of their food from local sources. The city has 13 farmers' market locations and an amazing diversity of fruit, berries, vegetables and nursery plants grown locally.

Getting Around

Along with Oakland and Philadelphia, Portland is one of the few cities in our study in which public ridership of mass transit has been increasing. Downtown's Fareless Square area helps make that easier, though where Portland has really excelled is in its regional coordination of city light rail and buses with outlying cities and the Portland International Airport.

Portland is a great place if you'd rather ride your bike. More than 10,000 Portlanders commute by bike, taking advantage of more than 700 miles of bicycle paths around the city. Portland led the largest 50 US cities in our study with a 2.8 percent bicycle commute-to-work rate.

Economic Factors

Portland's devotion to green building is known throughout the country. With 16 certified LEED buildings and 86 registered as of 2006, Portland has the most LEED buildings of any city. A $2.5 million fund for green building incentives in the commercial and residential markets suggests the city will continue its leadership in this area. The city is also committed to developing 100 percent renewable energy for city buildings by 2010, and is currently in negotiations for 51 megawatts of wind energy, to be generated in eastern Oregon.

In mid-2006, Portland passed an ambitious ordinance mandating that the city's gas stations provide 2.5 percent biodiesel fuel out of all diesel fuel sold by 2007, and 5 percent biodiesel fuel by 2010. Ty Kovatch, chief of staff for city council member Randy Leonard, who

Downtown Portland Bicycle Map.

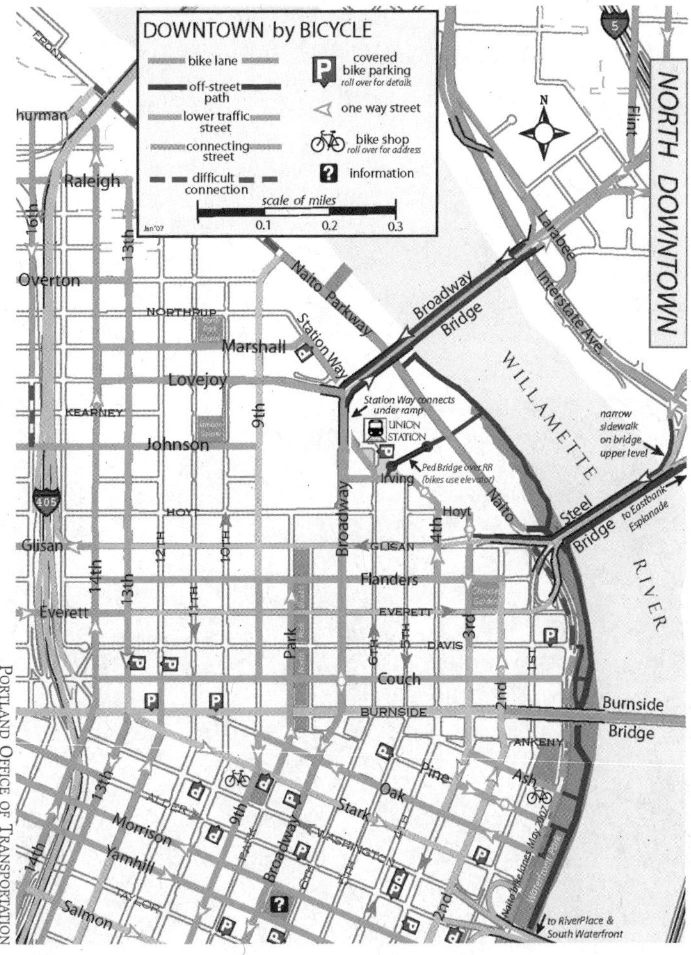

PORTLAND OFFICE OF TRANSPORTATION

sponsored the legislation, said, "The opportunity is for Portland to become the center of a legitimate alternative to the oil industry. We can even export it to China."

Said Mayor Tom Potter:

> We want to become less dependent on foreign oil. We are converting our diesel fleet to biodiesel so they can get around with less diesel from other countries. That's economic development; more money stays in the economy instead of going out of the country. In petroleum dollars, Oregon loses about $4 billion a year. That's significant. If we can reinvest $4 billion into the economy, think about what that would do for our economy, or any state's economy.

Thanks to the work of local real estate agent Kria Lacher and Meadows Group Realtors, Portland in 2007 will be rolling out the nation's first green multiple-listing service for the residential real estate market, with the system accommodating the detailing of green energy, materials and rating systems for prospective buyers of new and existing homes.

Portland is using its leadership to attract sustainability-oriented business gatherings as well as eco-tourists. Plenty of local businesses are in on the act, from restaurants offering organic, local ingredients; to the Green Meeting Industry Council; to stores selling environmental building supplies. One highlight is the Pearl District, a walkable mixed-use neighborhood that combines local businesses with renovated historic buildings such as the Jean Vollum Natural Capital Center. The center boasts a green roof, LEED certification and nonprofit tenants restoring salmon habitat as well as for-profits like Patagonia and Hot Lips Pizza, which uses local, sustainable ingredients for pizzas delivered by bicycle.

PORTLAND OFFICE OF SUSTAINABLE DEVELOPMENT

Portland neighborhood residents working together on City Repair.

Summary/Next Steps

With the momentum it's created around sustainable living, Portland is likely to continue to innovate. Its Office of Sustainable Development, unparalleled as a city management and communications office, is currently working with the Portland Development Commission to foster sustainable business practices throughout the city and expand the sustainable industries sector of the regional economy. There are few other medium-sized or large US cities that can match Portland in providing a sense of what the future can look like if citizens, businesses and public officials collaborate.

2

San Francisco, California

Still a Shining Example

Long admired for its innovative sustainability efforts, San Francisco has had particular success in the development of solar energy, recycling and large-scale composting, integrated pest management, bike transportation, green buildings, and local food systems.

Now that the city's sustainability plan is almost a decade old, new challenges are evident. Housing affordability (#49 out of the 50 cities) has become the most pressing issue. Since the dot-com boom drove up prices during the late 1990s, many lower-income and middle-class residents have been priced out of the housing market, and prices have not yet stabilized. Many Bay Area workers are forced by high home prices and rents to drive in from locations as far-flung as the Sierra Nevada foothills, three hours away.

The city's strong public transportation system has been slowly losing ridership. Traffic is getting bad again, with congestion ranking #47 on a metro area basis. Finally, San Francisco's earthquake risk poses a threat to the city's transportation system as well as to its power and water supplies.

Despite such challenges, San Francisco remains a standard-bearer for turning ambitious sustainability plans into reality.

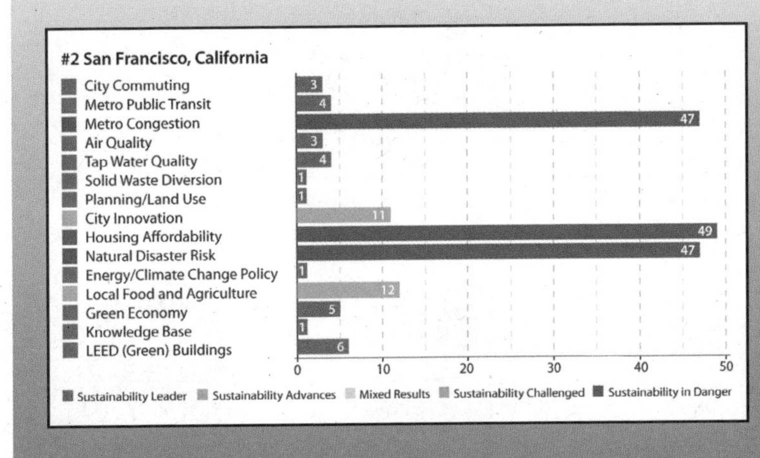

Healthy Living

If it weren't for Portland, San Francisco would clean up in this category. With clean air (#3), relatively good water (#4), a year-round local food system (#12) that's hooked into markets and restaurants showcasing local food, and the highest percentage (20%) of parkland among all 50 cities, it's a healthy place to live. These qualities have been factored into the value of every million-dollar two-bedroom home, whether or not people realize it.

Golden Gate Park, though not terribly eco-friendly, is beautiful and always entertaining. Dubbed by author Mark Reisner as "Borneo mated with Virginia," the park runs for three-plus non-native forested and flowered miles from the center of the city westward to its massive Ocean Beach terminus. The Presidio National Park, the former military base founded by Spanish soldiers and missionaries in 1776, is even larger — and it includes large-scale native plant and watershed restorations.

Getting Around

One of the best US cities for public transit commuter use (#4), San Francisco saw its ridership rate fall from 31 percent in 2000 to 29.6 percent in 2004. That trend should be reversed with the opening of the Third Street Light Rail Line in 2006. Walking to work and cycling to work are an everyday routine for many commuters. Largely because of the Bay Area Rapid Transit (BART) rail system, which opened in 1972, the Bay Area also ranks #4 for regional public transit ridership.

The region is served by several regional commuter ferry systems. These water transit options proved invaluable after the 1989 Loma Prieta Earthquake when the Oakland Bay Bridge was closed for repairs. Finally, a hard rail connects San Francisco and San Jose, and all Silicon Valley points between.

Prevalent mixed-land use promotes a neighborhood atmosphere. Corner of Grant Avenue and California Street.

COURTESY SFCVB/SETH AFFOUMADO

Mayor Gavin Newsom announced in mid-2006 a goal for the city to have 10 percent of all vehicle trips be made by bicycle, a goal that may sound unbelievable, considering the city had 2 percent bicycle ridership in 2005, but one that falls far short of some current European city bicycle commuter rates, such as more than 25 percent in Copenhagen.

Economic Factors

In 2005, Mayor Newsom was one of the first large-city mayors in the nation to publicly acknowledge the importance of local food, green buildings and other sustainability elements in the city's overall economic development strategy. "Sustainability is important not only for protecting citizens' health and ensuring a great quality of life here in San Francisco," Newsom said, "but also for boosting the local economy with jobs and services in everything from clean technologies to fresh food and green building products produced in California."

In renewable energy generation, San Francisco is a leader among North American cities. Since voters passed a $100 million solar bond measure, San Francisco has begun installing large solar systems, with about one megawatt now being generated atop its convention center and at a city wastewater plant. Tidal power generation from the ocean and San Francisco Bay, via a

A late spring morning at the Yerba Buena Gardens, one of San Francisco's many parks.

KAI-HUA CHENG

potential $10 million pilot project, is under study.

Clean technology business development is next on the city's agenda. Mayor Newsom has named a manager to head San Francisco's clean tech business attraction strategy, and to work with an advisory council. In 2005, the city's Board of Supervisors approved a payroll tax exemption for qualified clean tech companies doing business in San Francisco. With the bait set, can San Francisco become a center of renewable energy economic development?

On the rise all over town are green buildings, with San Francisco ranking #6 nationwide in green buildings per capita. As of early 2006, it had 10 LEED Certified buildings completed and 19 LEED Registered buildings in development. Out of its 1997 citizen-devised sustainability plan also came one of the country's first municipal green building ordinances, which now mandates LEED Silver certification for city construction. If better incentives were developed for the commercial and residential segments, the market would push LEED numbers even higher.

KAI-HUA CHENG

San Francisco residents shop fresh produce at the Ferry Building farmers' market.

Summary/Next Steps

San Francisco does a lot of things extraordinarily well: It's a healthy place to live with a city government that is leading the way toward sustainable alternatives in most categories. Other cities can learn a lot from San Francisco's model.

But like all big cities, San Francisco still faces some tough challenges. The high earthquake risk demands that the city government and San Franciscans together examine scenarios for disruption of transit, water supply and power on a regional scale.

Locally distributed power through solar or tidal systems can provide some insurance against an earthquake, as can continued development of alternative transit sources such as ferries and bicycles.

Affordable housing, however, is San Francisco's biggest sustainability albatross, with even professionals currently priced out of the market in many neighborhoods. Development of 6,000 more infill residential housing units near downtown in the Mission Bay area will provide some near-term relief, but much more housing development will be necessary to have any meaningful impact.

3

Seattle, Washington

Protecting a Promising Future

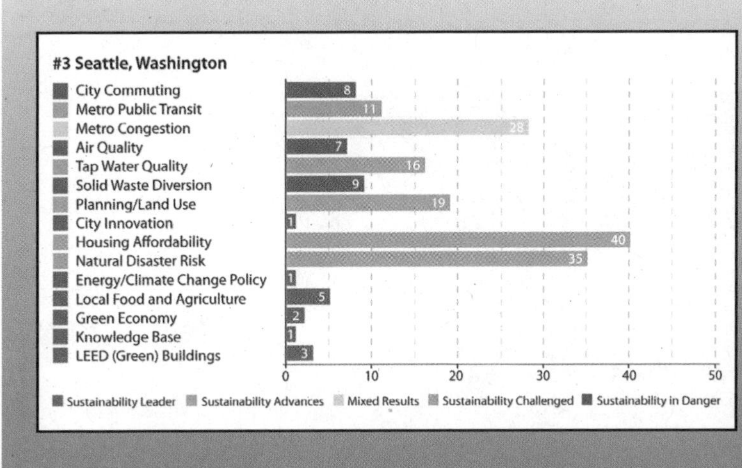

In Seattle, landscape and climate are more insistently part of the culture than in many other US cities, so it's no wonder that residents tend to develop an affinity for nature. Located between Puget Sound and Lake Washington, with dramatic sunsets and sweeping views of water, it's hard not to be drawn to the outdoors.

Easily accessed sailing, skiing, rock climbing, rafting, spelunking, hiking and camping are a few of the activities that make the city an outdoors person's paradise. This affinity for nature has been translated into leadership in sustainable living and policy.

Seattle's geographic placement also helps explain Mayor Greg Nickels's advocacy on climate protection, which grew directly out of his concern about preserving nearby glaciers and snowpack. In 2005, he was the first mayor to sign the US Mayors Climate Protection Agreement, which advances the goals of the Kyoto Protocol. He challenged mayors across the country to join him, and by late 2006, 330 mayors representing 53 million Americans had done so.

The city also finalized a climate action report in late 2006, detailing how city's residents and operations can reduce dependency on cars, while improving fuel efficiency and the use of biofuels. Seattle city government, according to Mayor Nickels in the report, has reduced its carbon emissions 60 percent from 1990 levels.

Plans are afoot to increase bus service, build more bicycle lanes, and change zoning to support more pedestrian-friendly communities as part of the multifaceted plan to address global warming locally. These moves will also, not coincidentally, create a healthier, more sustainable place to live.

Healthy Living

Seattle's air quality, which ranks #7, stays fresh thanks to Pacific breezes that filter through the Olympic Mountains. Water quality ranks #16, with nine contaminants, three of which exceed EPA recommendations. Superb local fruit, vegetables, flowers, meat and other products can be found at farmers' markets throughout Seattle; the famous Pike Place Market has inspired other markets across the country. About 70 community gardens dot the urban landscape, and Seattle ranks #5 overall in local food and agriculture.

Getting Around

Seattle ranks #8 in commuting and #11 in public transportation. While 61 percent of Seattleites drive to work alone, they do have viable alternatives. The state of Washington is a national leader in the use of biodiesel, which emits 78 percent less carbon dioxide and

A community garden in Seattle's High Point neighborhood.

Paul Symington

fewer greenhouse gases than gasoline. (The Washington State Ferries system is the largest user of biodiesel in the city.)

Two percent of commuters ride a bike to work, and 15 percent use public transportation on a daily basis. Though the city lacks a subway, it does have an excellent bus system. Many residents commute by ferry, and a light rail between downtown and the airport is slated to begin operations by 2009. The city has one of the leading big-city green fleets, with 46 percent of its more than 3,000 vehicles running on 20 percent biodiesel, electricity, hybrid or low-sulfur technologies.

Economic Factors

With a strong base of technology expertise from companies like Microsoft and Amazon.com, and a world-class educational institution in the University of Washington, Seattle is a major candidate to be a

Kayaking on Lake Union with the Space Needle visible in the distance.

leading city in clean technology development and implementation. Seattle's Office of Sustainability and the Environment has excelled in combining knowledge networks with information technology. Seattle has worked with its host county, King County, to help pioneer Environmentally Preferable Purchasing programs and with Starbucks, the University of Washington, the Seattle Technology Alliance and Pacific Northwest Laboratories to develop everything from climate impact research to a nascent clean tech cluster.

Seattle also ranks strong in green building at #3, offering a variety of incentives to encourage both residential and commercial green building. Its Green Home Remodel program offers free online guides to green remodeling — a lecture series, and free classes make it easy to add sustainability practices into the daunting remodel process.

Summary/Next Steps

Seattleites in both public and private life share a keen awareness of and commitment to the environment, and the city is at the forefront of sustainability. That hasn't left it without challenges. Mixed-use zoning, roadway congestion and tap water quality could all stand to be improved. Transit-oriented development using clean technologies would help address some of those challenges. The city's location makes it a good candidate for tidal energy generation, which both New York City and San Francisco have either implemented on a pilot basis or extensively studied. Overall, Seattle is on the right track toward creating a healthy and sustainable place for generations to come.

Seattle Gas Works Park, a public park on the site of a former Seattle Gas Light Company gasification plant.

Paul Symington

4

Chicago, Illinois

The Wind at Its Back

Chicago notched high scores nearly across the board: knowledge base (#1), city innovation (#5), energy and climate change policy (#5), commute to work (#6), and regional public transportation ridership (#2). The city has been moving toward a new type of urban environment since Mayor Richard M. Daley's administration began almost maniacally planting trees — about a half-million since Daley took office in 1989.

Mayor Daley's plan to make Chicago "the greenest city in America" soon blossomed into urban roof gardens, starting with City Hall in 2000. Throughout the city you can find attractive rooftop habitats for people and wildlife. Two and a half million square feet of planted rooftops now conserve building energy, filter rainwater and may nudge summertime temperatures down. Chicago has become the nation's living laboratory for studying the "urban heat island" effect, which can raise a city's temperatures 4 to 10 degrees on a scorching summer day. Lowering those temperatures by even a degree or two would save the city untold amounts of energy while reducing air-conditioning costs.

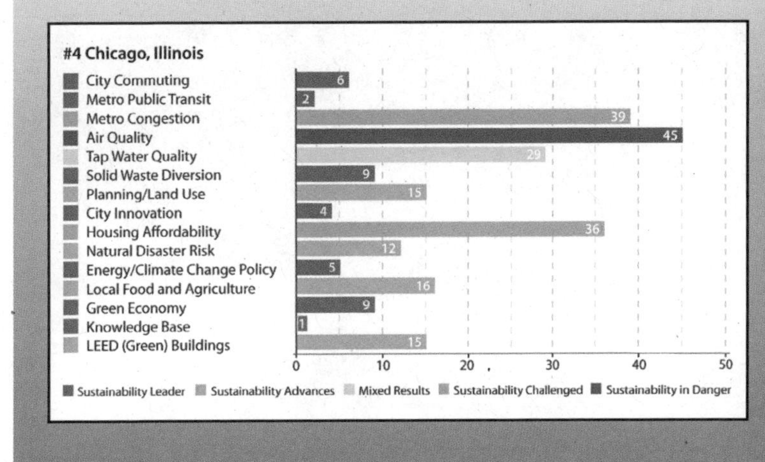

Chicago's forward-looking creativity extends to renewable energy, both solar and wind, which the city has been developing since the late 1990s.

Healthy Living

Lake Michigan permeates Chicago life. The lake is the place for recreation, and it's within blocks of everything from baseball's Wrigley Field, to Lincoln and Millennium parks, down to the University of Chicago's Hyde Park neighborhood on the South Side. Even Chicagoans who live miles from the lake are affected by climatic influences such

Millennium Park, a redeveloped section of abandoned industrial land, hosts one of the largest green roofs in the world.

City of Chicago/Peter J. Schulz

Muller and Muller Associates

as "lake effect" snowstorms. In warmer seasons, Lake Michigan is like a giant ice block, keeping temperatures cooler on the lakefront well into summer; conversely, during winter, temperatures are warmer near the water.

The extensive network of paths along the lake pulse with thousands of recreational runners, walkers and bike riders during summer, and provide bike commuters with dedicated pathways throughout the year.

Millennium Park, formerly an abandoned industrial site, is now one of the nation's top havens for tourists and locals alike. Anchored by a Frank Gehry-designed band shell and public interactive art installations, the park also features a giant green native plant rooftop, the nation's largest, over an underground garage and native plant educational displays.

Local food from a network of regional producers is available at 33 farmers' markets and at many restaurants and cafés. More than 400 city community gardens flourish, as neighborhood educational centers show how food, community and art can be mutually supportive.

Chicago is more challenged when it comes to the quality of its air and tap water. While Lake Michigan provides a plentiful source, Chicago tap water ranks below average at #29, with 17 contaminants resulting from industrial agriculture, other industries and urban runoff. Four contaminants are over the EPA's recommended levels.

Pritzker Pavillion in Millennium Park was designed by architect Frank Gehry.

Air quality ranks #45, with the South Side near the Calumet industrial region still showing signs of small and large particulate pollution from its cluster of manufacturing, especially during winter. Overall air quality can be sketchy on summer days, when smog-inducing ozone can cover the entire city all the way north to Wisconsin. To see how safe it is to exercise outdoors, check out the EPA's real-time air quality map at www.airnow.gov.

Getting Around

The "thousand-columned El," as writer Nelson Algren called it, makes its way through most neighborhoods of the city and into the suburbs. Chicago and its suburbs have one of the highest rates of public transit commuting in the nation (though commuter ridership fell from 26 percent in 2000 to less than 24 percent in 2004).

Economic Factors

Chicago has set a goal of having 20 percent of its energy come from renewable sources by 2010. With its renewable level currently at 2.5 percent, the city has a ways to go, but it is boosting the effort with the Chicago Center for Green Technology, a LEED Platinum building featuring a PV solar assembly company headquarters, and a green building demonstration center.

The ever-expanding metro area is surrounded in Illinois by industrial agriculture, but a renaissance of small producers from orchards and farms in Wisconsin, Indiana and Michigan is underway through the Local Organic Initiative. Fresh produce is becoming big business everywhere,

Pritzker Pavilion in Millennium Park designed by Frank Gehry in 2004.

MULLER AND MULLER ASSOCIATES

Free bike parking at Millennium Park.

from farmers' markets to supermarkets to upscale cafés. The Chicago area market buys $300 million in organic food each year, according to Sustain, a Chicago-based group that encourages sustainable economic development and local food sourcing.

JEREMY ATHERTON

A Critical Mass gathering of cyclists on the Daley Plaza, with Chicago City Hall in the background.

Chicago ranks #15 in green building, and its regional service and manufacturing economy is beginning to reap the benefits of solar power, wind energy, architecture, landscaping and innovative design technologies. Developers who construct green buildings are granted permits much more quickly than those who don't.

Summary/Next Steps

Chicago has taken the lead in building mainstream support for sustainability and green city programs. If it can continue on its current path while reversing declines in public transit and air quality, Chicago will be one of the world's urban sustainability models.

The city's reliance on Mayor Daley to lead the charge for being the "greenest city in the nation," however, does put its sustainability management programs at risk with any new mayor that may take over. But by that time, the Richard M. Daley green legacy might be firmly entrenched.

5

Oakland, California

Stepping out of the Shadows

Former mayor Jerry Brown, whose second term ended in 2007, initiated a plan to bring 10,000 new residents into a redeveloped city center. This tact is dramatically increasing the downtown population, reducing sprawl and making public transit more efficient — all while giving the city's urban center a dose of energy. Farmers' markets, community gardens and green buildings further support the city's move toward sustainability.

Oakland is one of the most ethnically diverse cities in the nation. While its expensive housing (#44) puts it out of reach for many Americans, it's more affordable than other Bay Area cities, including San Francisco and San Jose.

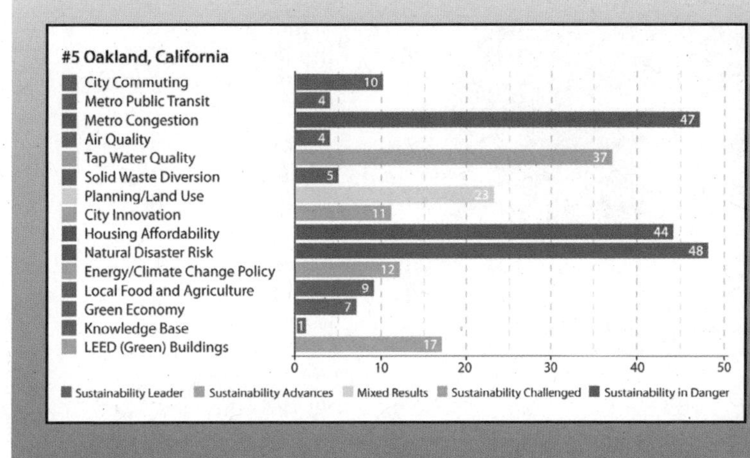

Healthy Living

Oakland's bayside location keeps its air cleaner (#4) than that of most American cities, with fresh Pacific breezes coming in through the Golden Gate and blowing straight at Oakland's port. Temperatures are pleasantly moderated by these cool breezes. The sun comes out more than it does in fog-enshrouded San Francisco, making Oakland a great setting for outdoor recreation and fitness.

On weekends and evenings, Oaklanders love to walk, jog, bike and play around Lake Merritt, a 140-acre tidal estuary adjacent to downtown, and in the other 65 parks and 29 regional parks covering more than 97,000 acres in Alameda and Contra Costa counties. The city's 8 farmers' markets and 36 community gardens support its #9 ranking for food and agriculture.

Water quality (#37) ranks below average, with 18 pollutants found in the water by the Environmental Protection Agency, 5 of which exceed the agency's recommended limits. If you live in Oakland, it's a good idea to filter your water.

Irene Bernadino/Lulu Lin

Irene Bernadino/Lulu Lin

A weekly downtown farmers' market provides fresh and organic food.

Getting Around

From 2000 to 2004, Oakland's public transit commuter use has increased more than in any US city we looked at, from 17 percent to 22 percent. Not only does this improve regional air quality, it also keeps money in the local economy that would otherwise leave the nation for imported oil.

The combined rate for biking and walking to work is just over 4 percent, which is below average for most of the larger, older US cities in our study. (This may reflect the number of people who commute across the bay to San Francisco or into Silicon Valley for jobs.) It will be interesting to see if the percentage improves with the continuing development of downtown residential neighborhoods.

Economic Factors

In conjunction with graduate students from the University of California in neighboring Berkeley, Oakland has created a plan to source 30 percent of its food locally. Oakland has demonstrated its leadership in supporting the expansion of farmers' markets, community gardens and school gardening programs.

Oakland ranks #17 in green building, with six registered and one certified green building, and derives two megawatts of solar power and 17 percent of its energy supply from renewable sources. This gives it a higher percentage of renewable energy than any other city analyzed in our city rankings. Oakland installed 1.1-megawatt solar arrays in 2005, one of the largest municipal installations in the nation.

In late 2006 the city passed a resolution, sponsored by councilmember Nancy Nadel, to study ways in which to make the city oil-free by 2020.

The city does face a serious earthquake risk, placing it at #48 for natural disasters, a lower ranking than even at-risk neighbors San Francisco and San Jose.

Summary/Next Steps

Oakland's innovations span several categories. Its plan to get 30 percent of the city's food from local sources, its strong public transportation infrastructure and its evolving city center reflect a commitment to sustainability. As part of an alliance with San Francisco, Berkeley and other Bay Area communities to jointly get half of their energy from renewable sources by 2017, Oakland has an opportunity to participate in a regional industry cluster that could one day serve the entire nation.

Oakland has a number of opportunities to strengthen its position. An important part of Oakland's vitality is its diversity, an asset it risks losing if it fails to create more affordable housing. Rising crime in low-income West Oakland is a continuing problem that affects all elements of the city's livability.

The city has also been challenged to retain jobs from its manufacturing base. Light manufacturing and/or assembly associated with solar and other renewable energy technology as part of Oakland's regional alliance would make an ideal match for the city's rail and port connections.

6

New York City, New York

Sustainability out of Necessity

New York City has many of the qualities that make many foreign cities livable: It's densely populated, with an exceptional subway and rail system and a diversity of local businesses that are most easily accessed by foot.

In many ways, New York City is an anomaly in the United States. The limitations of the city — its geographic boundaries and population density, which at 25,000 per square mile is more than six times that of #1 Portland — have forced it to be more sustainable than most US cities. Without an excellent public transportation system, plenty of parks and forward-thinking planning, it's hard to imagine so many people coexisting so successfully.

Said Mayor Michael R. Bloomberg, "Putting principles of sustainable development into practice is crucial to making sure that this city continues to be a place where people want to live and businesses want to grow in the 21st century. We know that our city must lead by example and we are working hard to make the 'Big Apple' a green apple."

Healthy Living

If you're a New Yorker, locally grown food is always close at hand.

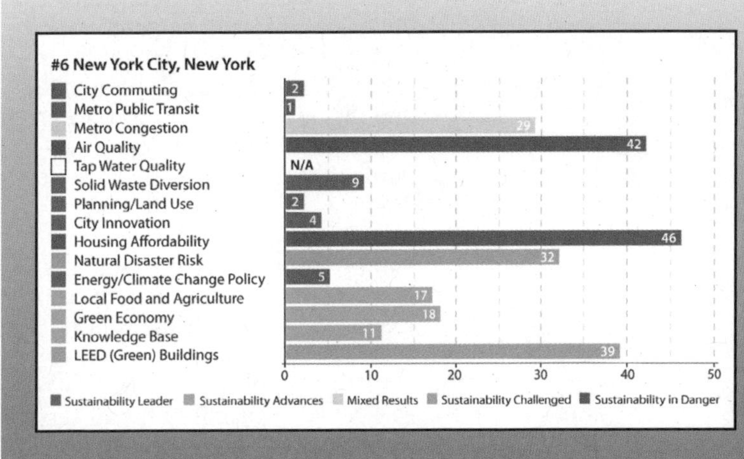

At any of the whopping 72 farmers' markets throughout the 5 boroughs, food is sold by the people who grew, raised, foraged or caught it. The city also has the largest urban gardening program in the nation, Green Thumb, which was founded in 1978 and now supports more than 700 community gardens.

Local food isn't the only thing helping New Yorkers stay healthy. The city ranks #3 for city land devoted to parks. These parks provide an easy way to escape the city's congestion. On a sunny day, you'll find throngs of people enjoying lunch, talking or going for a stroll.

New Yorkers also benefit from excellent drinking water from the Catskill and Croton area watershed, though we were unable to rank the water quality due to lack of currently available data. The Catskills are one of the largest protected urban watersheds, and the city's water supply is known to produce good-tasting and healthy tap water.

As can be expected in such a dense urban environment, New York City's air isn't so good, ranking #42. The city doesn't comply with Clean Air Act standards for ozone, and the air sometimes has dangerous levels of large and small particulate matter. New York's growing green municipal fleet and ultra-low sulfur diesel rules for garbage trucks, sightseeing buses, and city school buses should help reduce this danger somewhat.

New York City is necessarily one of the most sustainable cities in the US, because it's impossible to put so many people into such a small space without reducing their footprint on the earth.

Getting Around

The New York subway began service in 1904 — long before the automobile age — facilitating a high-density city with minimal sprawl. Less than a quarter of Manhattan residents own a car (the national average is 92 percent). In fact, people use as much gas in New York City today as the average American did in the 1920s. More than half of the population uses public transportation to commute to work. In addition to the subway, New York has the largest green municipal fleet in the country, 112,000 cyclists daily and the nation's busiest ferry system.

Economic Factors

Green skyscrapers? It's true. New York is one of the cities leading the pack in green building — especially skyscrapers. The new Bank of America headquarters in mid-town Manhattan is vying for the LEED Platinum standard, and will produce about half of its own energy while capturing rainwater for toilets from a rooftop harvesting system. In fact, the Skyscraper Museum had an exhibit in 2006 entitled "Green Towers for New York: From Visionary to Vernacular". The exhibit featured high-profile corporate headquarters, speculative office towers, green apartment blocks and mixed-use and institutional projects.

New York also has a burgeoning community of small businesses — media organizations, clothing designers, retail boutiques, furniture makers, dry cleaners, architecture firms — dedicated to green and sustainable alternatives. Locals "get" sustainability and are pioneering businesses and products to promote it.

Of course, New York is also among the least affordable cities in the study, ranking #46, with housing costs that are prohibitive for many. It's also a laggard when it comes to renewable energy, though the city is working on a pilot project that uses turbines in the East River to generate power from tidal energy.

Summary/Next Steps

New York City is necessarily one of the most sustainable cities in the United States, because it's impossible to put so many people into such a small space without reducing their footprint on the earth. People live in smaller spaces, require far less energy for driving, and tend to confine themselves to local shops in ways that have served as a model for mixed-use redevelopments across the nation.

Mayor Bloomberg's appointment of a Long-Term Planning and Sustainability director in mid-2006 was significant in that it placed a sustainability management structure across city functions into planning, which stands to have greater strategic impact than a "siloed" sustainability or environmental department. Other cities such as Chicago, San Francisco and Portland, Oregon are investigating similar cross-discipline approaches for city sustainability management.

On a number of more visible fronts, New Yorkers are pioneering more sustainable living solutions. The city's network of farmers' markets is impressive, its park space is enviable, and its focus on green building is positively inspiring. At the same time, New York faces ongoing challenges, most notably air pollution and congestion. No doubt, given its resources and the enterprising nature of its citizens, the city will find a way.

On a number of visible fronts, New Yorkers are pioneering more sustainable living solutions.

DANIEL SCHWEN / WIKIPEDIA / GNU FDL 1.2

Despite the bright lights, New York City has some of the lowest per capita energy use.

7

Boston, Massachusetts

It Only Gets Better

Set on a peninsula at the confluence of the Mystic, Charles and Chelsea rivers, Boston was a key port city in colonial days. The compact city aspires to create a future as bright as its past by improving an already efficient urban metabolism built on core strengths in public transit and planning.

Recent efforts at urban renewal have had positive environmental effects: A 12 percent reduction of carbon dioxide emissions and the addition of 320 acres of new parkland, according to Boston.com.

Said Brian Glascock, director of the Boston Environmental Department on *Barry Nolan's Nitebeat* show, "Every square foot that can be reclaimed and reused for some beneficial purpose, like a public park, is another amenity that we add to the city, and it certainly adds a lot of value to the properties around it. It's all part of a larger program to try and reclaim this paved, impervious surface throughout the city. More green space means more living material to filter the air, to filter the water."

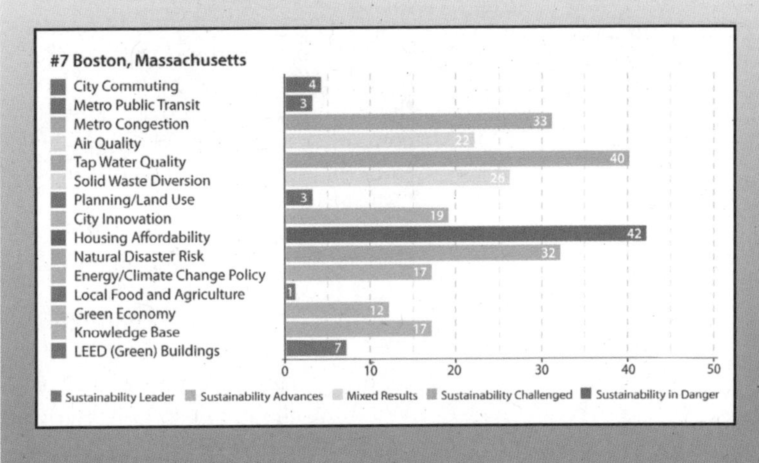

Healthy Living

Boston is a great place for parks, ranking #5. The Emerald Necklace, a series of linked parks that dates back to the early 19th century, brings together botanical gardens and shaded river walks.

Boston ranks #1 for local food and agriculture. Community gardens are thriving, thanks to nonprofits like the Boston Natural Areas Network, which helps neighborhoods establish, organize and maintain gardens. Farmers' markets (13 and counting) continue to sprout up around the city. The Food Project runs an urban farm that teaches agriculture to young people and helps feed the city's underprivileged.

Air quality ranks a slightly above average #22, but water quality, rated "poor" by the Natural Resources Defense Council's urban tap water study, comes in at #40.

Boston is on the road to becoming a more sustainable city, with a city government committed to sustainable practices.

Getting Around

In Boston, urban development is informed by a dense mixed-use city center served by public transit rather than freeway access; the city ranks #3 in terms of planning. And its public transit service is superb.

The subway, called "the T," is the oldest in the country, but Boston keeps it current. Bus routes are extensive and include express runs that use reserved highway lanes. A commuter rail moves people to and from the outlying metro with free transfers to subways and buses inside the city. As is the norm in the United States, commuter lines share rail with freight haulers.

All modes of transit go to the airport, including the ferries that routinely crisscross Boston Harbor. More transit stations are in the works, and lines are being extended. A third of all Bostonians use public transportation and over 8 percent walk to work, helping the city rank #3 in commute to work.

Economic Factors

Boston is also one of the nation's leaders in green building (#7). The Green Building Task Force provides cash incentives for construction and renovation projects that demonstrate LEED ambitions. One such building, the John W. McCormack Post Office and Courthouse, is an Art Deco colossus built during the Great Depression. It's now aiming for LEED certification with upcoming renovations including an all-shrubbery green roof.

In late 2006, Boston became the first major US city to change its zoning laws to require that all new buildings of more than 50,000 square feet obtain a minimum of LEED certified status.

One of the lead agencies in Boston's green technology push is the Massachusetts Technology Collaborative, which, in addition to fomenting innovation in general, runs a Renewable Energy Trust. Each month, a small percentage of power bill revenues go into the trust, which supports green building, alternative fuel research and public outreach. This program and others like it place Boston far ahead of the curve in terms of renewable energy use, with more than 8 percent of the city's energy coming from renewable sources.

Summary/Next Steps

Boston is on the road to becoming a more sustainable city, with a city government committed to sustainable practices. Based on the success of programs in European cities and Chicago, the city has begun a green roofs program, including planning for a green roof on city hall.

There are several opportunities that could promote an even better quality of life for the city's residents. Improvement in both air and water quality would make the city a healthier place to live. About half of the city relies on heating oil, most of which is imported and vulnerable to world market forces. And Boston has no green-house gas reduction goals or tracking mechanism. Portland and San Francisco could both serve as models for improvement in that area.

8

Philadelphia, Pennsylvania

City on the Move

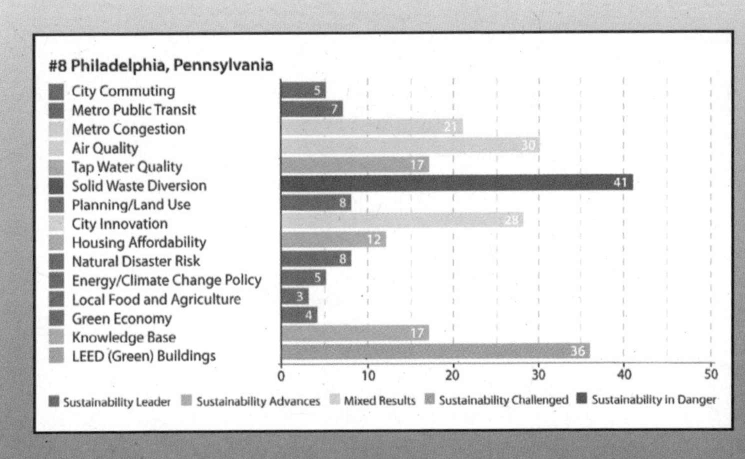

Look beyond Philadelphia's patchwork of abandoned manufacturing sites, and you'll find a city that's emerging as a solid model of how cities can address environmental impact while maintaining vibrant local neighborhoods and culture.

The "Brooklyn effect" seems to be happening in Philadelphia. From warehouses to old industrial sites, artists and young families are moving back into central Philadelphia neighborhoods. The challenge with modern urban renewal is how to enrich the city centers without displacing longtime residents, many who work in service industries. Cities must remain affordable for all in order to be truly sustainable.

Philadelphia ranks strong in many categories, including transportation (tied for #2 in overall mobility), local food and agriculture (#3), and energy and climate change policy (#5).

Healthy Living

Philadelphia is at the forefront of the urban local food renaissance. Its 18 farmers' markets, all of which accept food stamps, offer a huge variety of produce and fruit from the surrounding Amish and Pennsylvania Dutch farms. Tasting a sweet potato pie from Reading Terminal Market, a longtime local food and craft market from 1892, is one of the best ways to experience a longtime staple of the city's African-American community. And the White Dog Cafe, featuring Judy Wickes's locally procured organic food, is the cultural center for urban-rural linkages statewide, with its breakfast talks, movies and weekly community gatherings.

The Philadelphia Green program, sponsored by the Pennsylvania Horticultural Society, helps support more than 20 of the city's 465 community gardens in addition to leading numerous innovative large-scale public space greening and watershed protection initiatives. Philadelphia Green aims to increase local property values while addressing with fresh, locally grown produce issues like food security and the more than 50 percent of the city's children that are overweight.

The city's water is relatively good (#17), coming from the Schuylkill River watershed. Air quality ranks slightly below average at #30, with moderate ozone and small particulate pollution. With about 12 percent of Philadelphia's city land devoted to parks, green space is a strength (#11). Fairmount Park alone is over 9,200 acres, or more than ten times the size of New York City's Central Park, and it's within walking distance for all of the city's 2.4 million residents.

Getting Around

Philadelphia's public transportation rates are among the highest in the nation, with 27 percent using it to get to work.

Philadelphia's public transportation rates are among the highest in the nation, with 27 percent using it to get to work. It's one of the few cities in our study (Portland and Oakland are two others) in which public transit rates are improving — in 2004 a higher percentage of people were using public transit than in 2000. Thanks to its robust public transportation system, Philadelphia's mobile energy use is in good shape; in a separate SustainLane index, it ranked as the #5 city best prepared for an oil crisis.

Philadelphians can also easily walk or ride bikes to get around, with 6.5 percent of people walking to work. The city also sponsors signage and walking maps prepared specifically for pedestrians, with at-a-glance figures for distances and estimated times. Philly makes the top ten for city planning, with much less sprawl than the average American city.

Economic Factors

SustainLane's sustainable economic measures (farmers' markets, green building, clean tech incubation and health and green business directories) place Philadelphia at #4. In addition to the farmers' markets, Philly has an active Sustainable Business Network with healthy and green business listings, though the city came in at #36 in LEED buildings per capita, with only two LEED certified buildings and five registered as of early 2006.

City clean technology development partners include Kronosport, which makes some of the city's electric vehicles, and Philadelphia University, with which the city is applying for a patent for energy-efficient insulating walls for low-income housing.

Summary/Next Steps

Philadelphia's sustainability planning is in its early stages, but it's clearly on the right path. Citizen groups, state and local government agencies, and academic and scientific institutions sponsored public sustainability forums throughout 2006 to get citizens' ideas about how to move forward. The Philadelphia Urban Sustainability Forum hosts a blog focused on the same efforts.

One big opportunity that Philadelphia has missed so far is renewable energy. It may find inspiration by looking to Chicago, Boston and many West Coast cities.

Solid waste diversion was under 10 percent, one of the nation's lowest rates; the lack of recycling in the city has been challenging for those who want to but can't recycle at the office and in public places. Single-stream recycling, which has become an effective approach that leading California cities have perfected, may be a good option for a populace that has not yet fully participated in the circular material economy.

(Right) *Downtown Philadelphia as seen from the Philadelphia Museum of Art.*

(Below) *Local Philadelphia Italian market. Small locally owned food markets in mixed-use residential neighborhoods offer a more sustainable and accessible alternative to supermarkets that must be driven to.*

Jeffrey M. Vinocur / CreativeCommons 2.5

Derek Ramsey / commons.wikimedia.org/wiki/Image

9

Denver, Colorado

On the Fast Track

Located on the high plains at the base of the Rocky Mountains, Denver is geographically unique. As the only large city within a 600-mile area, halfway between the Midwest and West Coast, it has become a major center for the storage and distribution of goods and services.

Denver was one of the few cities in the country to boom during the oil crisis of the 1970s. At a time when almost every city's downtown experienced blight and "white flight," Denver was building skyscrapers and actually putting money into its downtown. But when oil prices fell, so did Denver's economy. A generation later, Denver experienced a similar boom and bust with the rise and fall of the high-tech industry, much of which was based in its surrounding suburbs. These experiences have led the city to pursue a more diversified and sustainable economic future.

With the leadership of Mayor John Hickenlooper, Denver is at the forefront of a new economy — one based on sustainability. A petroleum geologist by training, he left that industry to become a brewmaster, in part, he says, "Because microbrew was the more profitable liquid fuel in those days." One of his major concerns is minimizing the impact of an oil crisis. He realizes that when oil prices rise, they affect not only the cost of driving, but also the cost of producing and transporting goods and services, and consequently the entire economy.

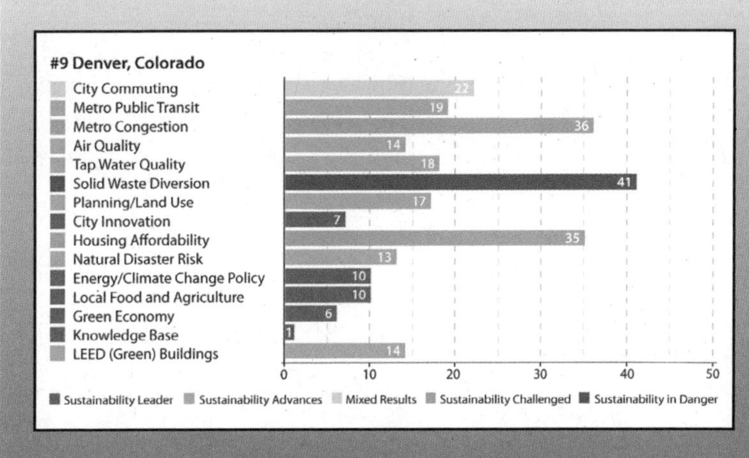

To address these issues, Hickenlooper launched the Denver Sustainable Development Initiative, a collaborative effort to reduce waste; improve air and water quality; and promote multi-modal, transit-oriented land use, energy conservation, green building, solar energy and reduction of greenhouse gas emissions. The city's GreenPrint Denver program, a collaborative planning effort among government, thought leaders, business and citizens groups, was launched in July 2006.

Healthy Living

Both water quality and public park availability need improvement, though air quality receives a relatively high ranking. The South Platte River Water Quality Initiative was created to address Denver's tap water quality (#18) and supply. This multi-partner program provides education and outreach to measurably improve water quality in the Denver watershed. The fresh mountain air maintains high quality (#14) for a city of this size. Though parks in Denver are conveniently located near downtown, shopping and restaurants, Denver falls in the bottom half of the study for its overall city land devoted to parks, ranking #29.

With 8 farmers' markets, Denver residents benefit from a good supply of locally grown food; it ranks #10 for food and agriculture.

With 8 farmers' markets, Denver residents benefit from a good supply of locally grown food; it ranks #10 for food and agriculture. In many cities, the ability to grow one's own food, or even to see how food is grown, is becoming a rarity. But Denver Urban Gardens (DUG) is providing that opportunity for hundreds of low- to moderate-income urban neighborhoods throughout the city. DUG operates or supports over 50 community gardens. Through the gardens, residents supplement their diet with food that they raise themselves.

Getting Around

Denver currently ranks #22 for commuting and #19 for public transportation, but these rankings should dramatically increase soon. In 2004, the public passed FasTracks, a $4.7 billion ballot initiative to increase light rail, commuter rail and bus rapid transit service. It even includes a ski train for folks to access the nearby Rockies resorts. The initiative was the largest local transit funding measure in the history of the nation.

Many recent articles attribute the increase of commercial activity downtown, especially retail, to light rail and other public transportation. Apparently, more Denver area residents, employees and visitors have poured into the urban core. According to an article on Denver light rail in *Light Rail Now*, "wildly popular rail lines are drawing people who never considered taking the bus." The first rail lines in 2001 drew 43 percent more riders than projected. As Denver's director of planning, Peter Park, noted, "It is easier to add light rail cars than it is to widen highway lanes."

The city has made a commitment to alternative-fueled vehicles, which account for 31 percent of its present vehicle fleet, one of the highest percentages in the nation. The Mile High City has made a commitment to have a 100 percent alternative fueled city fleet by the end of 2007.

Economic Factors

Mayor Hickenlooper is devoted to incorporating sustainable measures into every aspect of Denver's emerging economy. One study examined the petroleum used by the city and the potential impacts of oil price spikes on the city budget. Now the city is looking into more ways to use alternative fuel. Several pioneering projects have been completed and others are in the pipeline.

Denver International Airport realized unprecedented success in 2004 by becoming the first major American airport to become ISO 14001 certified for its Environmental Management System. Other innovative projects include the anticipated installation of solar panels on the south-facing roof of the Colorado Convention Center. A city proposal went out in mid-2006 for the nation's first municipally owned urban solar power plant to provide power to a jail.

As a leader in sustainability, Denver is bringing other cities together. At the Denver Green Cities Forum in November 2005, sustainability directors from Portland, Seattle, Salt Lake City, Oakland and Chicago met to discuss best practices and strategies, and another event is planned for 2007.

Summary/Next Steps

Denver has placed itself in a unique position to lead the nation in transportation-based, economically focused sustainability approaches. The leadership of a passionate, well-liked mayor with a strong vision practically guarantees that Denver will be able to achieve its goals. Its efforts to wean itself from automotive dependence should be an inspiration to sprawling cities that think it's too late to do anything about their failing — or almost non-existent — public transit systems.

Denver has additional opportunities. Less than 1 percent of the city energy mix uses renewable energy. The city ranks poorly in recycling, diverting less than 10 percent

Downtown Denver gathering.

of its solid waste from the landfill. Although green building incentives are in the planning process, they have not yet been instituted. Further attention could also be paid to increasing the city's local food supply and widening its distribution. But given the city's record to date, it's clear that Denver is on the fast track to a more sustainable future.

Denver is looking beyond the sunsetting of the oil economy.

DAG PEAK / WIKIPEDIA / CREATIVECOMMONS 2.5

10

Minneapolis, Minnesota

Clean Air, Big Plans

Minneapolis charms residents and visitors alike with its graceful tree-lined parkways, lakes, multiethnic restaurants, and vibrant arts and music scene. Then there's the winter — endless days of numb fingers, gray sludge corroding your car and soaking your shoes, and high energy bills. In recent years, though, there hasn't been enough snow to get a good cross-country ski race going. During the winter of 2005-2006, unprecedented numbers of ice fishers' cars fell through the ice on city lakes.

Minneapolitans are concerned about the warming winters, and the city is doing its part to lower its energy impact: In 1999, Minneapolis became one of the first US cities to adopt sustainability indicators.

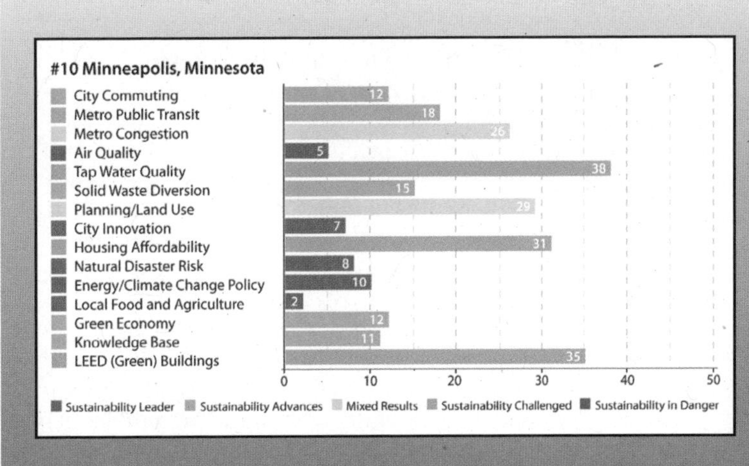

Healthy Living

Can you canoe? If so, the Chain of Lakes lets you cruise through channels to several city lakes, which are also popular swimming holes. All year round, people throng Minneapolis's parks. Cyclists and in-line skaters have over 80 miles of trails to choose from, and in the winter, the parks are favorite spots for sliding, cross-country skiing, and ice skating.

Enjoying the outdoors is easier when the air is clean, as it is in Minneapolis (#5). You might want to think twice (and install a good carbon filter) before drinking the tap water, though. The water, from the Mississippi, not only smells an awful lot like chlorine, but when last tested contained 21 contaminants, 5 of which were over the EPA limit (#38).

Plants and gardens thrive in the city. Minneapolis has 100 community gardens and counting. These gardens aren't just a fun hobby. According to Lori Olson of the city's Environmental Department, "The Youth Farm and Market Project . . .

plays an important role in nurturing relationships between urban youth and the earth around them by letting them grow, cook, eat and sell healthy food." All but one of Minneapolis's farmers' markets accept WIC vouchers, enabling more residents to enjoy the bounty of this rich farming region.

Getting Around

Minneapolis has bold plans to reduce greenhouse gas emissions, increase renewable energy use and reduce homelessness.

With an impressive network of bicycle commuter trails, Minneapolis ranks #2 in bike commuting, with 2.3 percent pedaling to work. The city ranks #18 in overall public transportation use and healthy commuting (carpooling, biking and walking). That might sound like a good showing, but fewer people walked or cycled to work in 2004 (3%) than in 2000 (7%).

Likewise, more people drove alone to work in 2004 (65%) than in 2000 (62%). Countering this trend is a light rail system launched in 2005. Ridership has far exceeded expectations and should help get increasing numbers of commuters out of their cars, which will in turn help reduce energy consumption.

Minneapolis is one of 17 business districts in the country to earn the EPA's "Best Workplaces for Commuters" seal for providing carpool coordination and transit subsidies to employers. Residents can also participate in local carshare programs. Minneapolis could further benefit by greening its fleet of city vehicles, less than 5 percent of which currently run on alternative fuels.

Economic Factors

Not only do community gardens and farmers' markets make for healthier people, they benefit the local economy as well. In 2006, the city opened the Midtown Global Market to promote ethnically diverse food and discourage shopping at "big box" stores, featuring more than 50 local, independent vendors.

Speaking of big boxes, Minneapolis invented the mall, and the country's largest, the Mall of America, is the most widely visited landmark in the Twin Cities area. However, many residents are fed up with driving through congested streets to spend their dollars at chain stores that sap dollars from the local economy. A few communities, including the Linden Hills neighborhood, have organized campaigns to support local businesses. The city as a whole provides links to green businesses through the Twin Cities Green Guide.

Minneapolis leads the Midwest in green energy, with 4 percent of its total energy coming from renewables. Wind is a growing industry, along with solar and biomass. By 2008, the city pledges to increase its renewable energy use to 10 percent. The city lags behind others in green building — to date, it has no LEED certified buildings, although some public buildings conform to less stringent state green building guidelines.

Minneapolis also offers a few green building incentives, including incentives for green roofs and walls, a density bonus, and storm water utility fee credits, but these piecemeal measures pale in comparison to the energy savings ensured by buildings built to LEED standards. The Green Institute offers tours to the public on green building and has developed a few green enterprises that can serve as models for developing larger-scale efforts.

Summary/Next Steps

Minneapolis has strong leadership in sustainability planning from both Mayor R.T. Rybak and the city council. The city has bold plans to reduce greenhouse gas emissions, increase renewable energy use and reduce homelessness. These important efforts may take years to bear fruit, while in the short term Minneapolis faces other challenges: among them a widening divergence between the priorities of urban dwellers and the rural population, and sprawling suburbs. Chances are that a city that has survived extended periods of 25-below-zero weather will continue to thrive throughout the next century.

City of Minneapolis

Down the Mississippi River in Minneapolis.

11

Baltimore, Maryland

A Port Town Reinventing Itself

Baltimore's identity as a working-class port town is undergoing a transformation, as the downtown is revitalized, empty lots are converted to community gardens, and shipping centers are transformed into waterfront residential neighborhoods. The renovated waterfront is now also home to museums, cruise operations, retail stores and restaurants. It's an affordable city that offers a strong public transportation system, abundant options for locally grown food and a variety of attractive public parks.

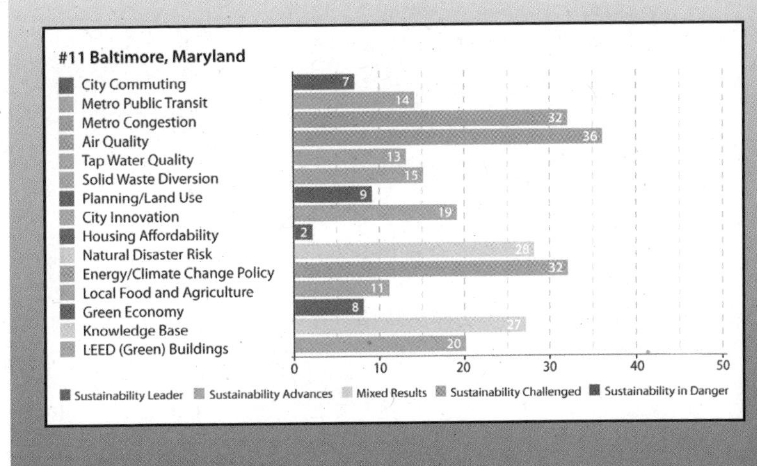

Healthy Living

In 2000, Baltimore had 14,000 vacant lots. In response to this blight, the city's Parks and People Foundation created the Baltimore Grows project, which has helped community groups create and maintain more than 250 community gardens on city-owned vacant property. Community members, many from low-income neighborhoods, work on the gardens and learn valuable skills in creating, maintaining and harvesting food resources. Produce from the gardens is sold to farmers' markets and restaurants. Four farmers' markets throughout the city are another source for fresh, locally grown produce, meats and specialty goods.

In another promising initiative, the city has committed to the Urban Tree Canopy Goal project, which aims to double the number of trees in the city over the next 30 years. This should improve air quality (#36) and help pedestrians and bicyclists keep cool.

Outdoor activities are quite accessible, and the city's percentage of parkland ranks #14 (parkland is a subcategory of planning, where Baltimore is also strong at #9). Chief among the many parks is Druid Hill Park. The second-largest urban park in the United States, residents heavily use its shady lawns, rolling hills,

Community gardens, local food, good public transportation and affordability all make Baltimore an excellent place for healthy living.

forestland and numerous streams and lakes.

Getting Around

Baltimore ranks #6 in overall mobility (which includes congestion, city eco-friendly commuting to work, and regional public transportation), in part because of a commitment to public transportation that dates back to the 1890s. A subway debuted in 1983, light rail in 1992, and both have been highly successful. Twenty percent of Baltimoreans use public transit to get to work (#8). Because of the city's high density, walking is also a great commute option: 6.5 percent walk to work. The city council has supported a campaign to calm traffic and create more pedestrian-friendly measures. Most citizens (58%) drive to work alone, but that rate is low compared to the rest of the nation's cities.

The Plug-In Baltimore campaign is part of a new nationwide program to encourage local government, education, business and environmental organizations to consider the future purchase of flexible-fuel plug-in hybrid vehicles. Baltimore was one of the first cities to join the campaign. Less than 1 percent of the city's fleet vehicles, however, currently use alternative fuels.

Economic Factors

With a relatively low cost of housing and a high average income, Baltimore is the second most affordable city in our rankings.

Like some other Eastern cities, Baltimore excels in certain healthy living areas and transportation, but doesn't score as well in the area of green economy. There are no incentives for green building (the city is #20 in LEED buildings) and 0 percent of its energy mix comes from renewable sources. The Chesapeake Bay Region chapter of the Business Alliance for Local Living Economies supports local businesses with networking and directories.

Summary/Next Steps

Community gardens, local food, good public transportation and affordability all make Baltimore an excellent place for healthy living. The city is also a leader in urban watershed protection, with the Baltimore Watershed Agreement aimed at restoring the decline of Chesapeake Bay water quality.

The city could benefit by focusing on developing incentives for green building and clean technology development. By doing so, Baltimore has an opportunity to create an even healthier environment for its residents and visitors.

12

Washington, DC

Leading by Example

The city of Washington, DC conjures images more granite than green, more power than produce. But can the capital city get more sustainable? Yes, and D.C. already has the grades to prove it, as well as signs of further improvement ahead.

Washington is the planned city par excellence, an intentional space of ceremony and symmetry. Buildings taller than 160 feet are forbidden, and the resulting vistas are broad, punctuated by domes and spires. City layout is rectilinear with diagonal streets radiating from key squares. Avenues — long, straight and lined with trees — arrange unbroken fields of view to better highlight monuments and monumental architecture.

Today, 550,000 people live in the company town for the colossal federal government. Many more live in the suburbs. The traffic is terrible — Washington's congestion ranks #46. But the city also showcases some of the leading sustainable practices in the nation. Some of these efforts are initiated upstairs by the feds, some come from city management, and some come from DC natives who are gradually relocalizing city neighborhoods.

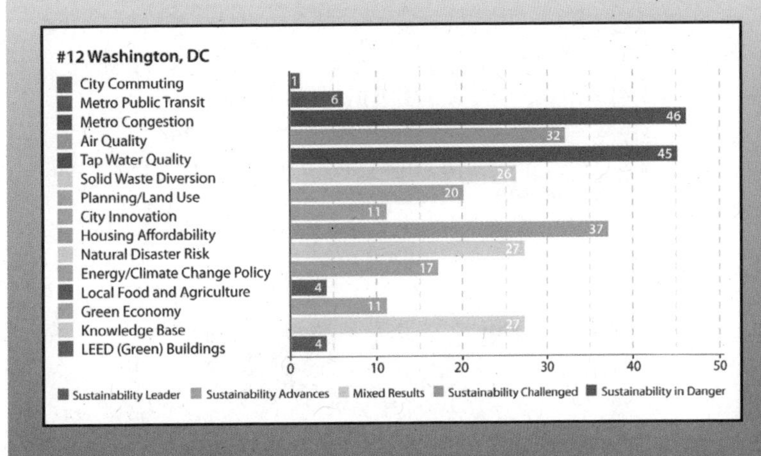

Healthy Living

First, the bad news. Washington, DC ranks near last (#45) in water quality. In 1994, testing showed widespread lead pollution affecting over 23,000 homes. Since then, WASA has treated city water and initiated a lead-line replacement program, reducing lead content in recent tests. The EPA continues to monitor the problem, but as of August 2006, EPA reports that sampling indicates DC water no longer exceeds federal "action levels."

On the bright side, the city ranks high (#4) in local food development, a combined measure of farmers' markets and community gardens. The city is second only to Honolulu for farmers' markets per capita. Many seasonal markets throughout the city connect consumers with farmers from Pennsylvania, Maryland and Virginia. Some of the markets are hosted by the USDA, which publicly encourages the direct marketing of local foods. Thanks in part to its superb design, the city also boasts an abundance of natural space, with over 19 percent of the city devoted to parks.

Getting Around

Of the cities studied by SustainLane, most of the ones with good public transit systems adopted subways or elevated trains well before the introduction of motorcars. That's why the success of Washington's subway system, which opened decades after most of the country had converted to suburbia and superhighways, is especially impressive.

Today, this metro system of rail and extensive bus routes make up the city's public transit array. Nearly 34 percent of city residents use public transportation to commute, and the federal district ranks #6 in public transportation. An impressive 11 percent of residents walk to work, a higher percentage than anywhere else in our study. In all, DC ranks #1 for its diverse mix of well-used commuting options.

A noteworthy DC innovation (also practiced in the San Francisco Bay Area) is instant carpooling, or "slugging," in which people needing rides wait at bus stops and drivers needing bodies to qualify for the carpool lane pull up advertising their destinations. No agency governs slugging. It's a surprising and encouraging practice in a city so characterized by officialdom.

Economic Factors

Headquartered here, the US Green Building Council oversees programs such as LEED certification, currently the national standard for sustainable construction. LEED building has been embraced by many government agencies, so it isn't surprising that LEED technology is showcased throughout Washington, DC. The city ranks #4 in our study for green building.

But some of the city's most inspiring achievements in green building fall outside of official certification. GreenHOME is a grassroots nonprofit that, in partnership with

Passengers board a train at Metro Station, Washington D.C.

Courtesy Washington, D.C. Convention and Tourism Corporation

Habitat for Humanity, advocates for homes that are both sustainable and affordable. In 1998, GreenHOME completed a single-family home that saves energy and reduces waste; its low-impact construction used recycled materials and cost less than $65,000. The house was donated to a low-income family.

Summary/Next Steps

Partially in response to the lead in its drinking water, Washington, DC created a Department of Environment in 2005. The department concerns itself with sustainability and assumes functions previously scattered throughout the departments of Health, Public Works, Transportation and the Water and Sewer Authority. It promises to develop a green fleet of city vehicles using hybrid and natural gas technology, and to investigate ways to reduce the city's energy footprint.

This nascent outfit may very well shape the development of a city traditionally intent on characterizing American power, governance and responsibility. Its opportunity is momentous: to reach out to community innovators, recognize the value of unfamiliar technologies, and render more of Washington, DC — the neighborhoods, highways, and sewers, not just the monuments and historic buildings — a living symbol of national achievement.

Washington, D.C. has the highest walk-to-work rate of any city in the United States.

Washington, DC Convention and Tourism Corporation

13

Sacramento, California

Capital Ideas

Sacramento has a lot going for it. Locals enjoy its proximity to two rivers, the Sierra Nevada Mountains, and the San Francisco Bay Area. These geographic blessings are also a curse: high pollutant counts and 100-degree temperatures in the summer can make easy breathing a challenge and outdoor exercise dangerous, and its neglected levees mean some parts of the city are vulnerable to flooding. But the city has a number of initiatives to address these challenges, including a light rail system, many new urban infill projects and an impressive array of solar energy installations.

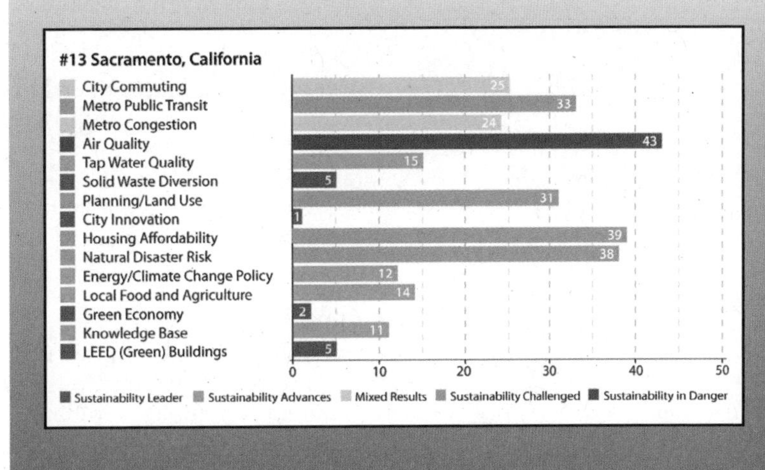

Healthy Living

Sacramento has poor air, ranking #43. Before exercising and spending time outdoors, residents should check the EPA's Spare the Air website (www.airnow.gov) for local pollutant forecasts (you might also sign up for the "Air Alert" e-mail forecast). Sacramento's water ranks considerably better, at #15.

As befits a city that celebrates its NBA basketball team by ringing cowbells, local produce can be found throughout town at a variety of farmers' markets. There are, however, fewer organic stalls than in Sacramento's neighbors to the west, Oakland and San Francisco. The conventionally raised produce reinforces regional agricultural practices that pollute the city's tap water with pesticides.

Six percent of city land is set aside for parks, ranking #33. The city's Discovery Trail, popular with joggers and bicyclists, follows the American River for 54 miles from downtown Sacramento. The city also has an impressive urban forest that the Sacramento Tree Foundation aspires to double in size in order to help improve air and water quality and reduce overall energy use.

Sacramento has a number of strengths to build on. It's doing an excellent job diverting waste, has a strong rating in green building, and is a leader in solar energy.

Getting Around

Despite its successful light rail project — including new extensions to Folsom that opened in 2005 — public transit remains an issue in Sacramento. About 3 percent of residents use public transit to commute, while 1.4 percent commute by bicycle and 2.9 percent walk to work. Carpooling is slightly above average for US cities at about 11 percent. Still, almost 78 percent of residents drive alone to work, contributing to the region's air pollution.

However, public transit ridership has been climbing steadily, and Sacramento plans to continue extending the light rail system. Don't be surprised to see non-automobile commute percentages rise over the next few years.

Economic Factors

A government town with a growing high-tech presence, Sacramento is home to numerous projects in both solar energy and green building that predate statewide mandates. The city ranks #5 in LEED buildings per capita, including the 25-story LEED Gold Certified California EPA headquarters.

Sacramento also has what might be the largest base of residential and business solar industry systems in the nation, with more than 1,000 installations. The Sacramento Municipal Utility District (SMUD) offers incentives not only for photovoltaic solar, but also for concentrating solar, wind energy, biomass and other renewables.

In fact, SMUD takes one of the most complete sustainability systems approaches found in any American city by offering local home buyers options to buy Zero Energy Homes and by providing free shade trees. A tree benefit calculator will even estimate the energy savings and carbon sequestration of your mature shade trees.

With such attention paid to sustainable economic development, it's no surprise that Sacramento ranks #2 (tied with Seattle) for overall green economy indicators.

Sacramento ranks #38 for natural disaster risk. In addition to the aged levees, Folsom Dam, perched above Sacramento, sits atop the federal Bureau of Reclamation's ominous-sounding "Safety Priority" list.

Summary/Next Steps

Sacramento has a number of strengths to build on. It's doing an excellent job diverting waste, has a strong rating in green building, and is a leader in solar energy.

Both of the city's biggest weaknesses, air pollution and congestion, are related to sprawl. The pollution is compounded by nearby agricultural production that relies heavily on pesticides, as well as geographic features that cause air pollution to stick around rather than blow away. Finding alternatives to car use and reckoning with the pollution caused by industrial agriculture would help create a healthier city. Several downtown mixed-use development projects in various stages of planning should take some cars off the road while creating a more vital urban center. Additional mixed-use development as well as continued investment in light rail should help the city deal with its challenges.

14

Austin, Texas

A Pioneer

Austin was a pioneer in green building during the late 1980s and early 1990s, when most cities gave little thought to the consequences of how much energy, water and materials were used during construction, use and demolition. With the help of Gail Vittori and visionary local architect Pliny Fisk, Austin developed a whole rating system and program around the concept.

More recently, Mayor Will Wynn has led the charge for renewable energy, making Austin a national center for innovation. The Clean Energy Incubator is a leading consortium of business, academic — the University of Texas has its main campus here — and state government leaders devoted to helping about eight young clean-energy companies succeed.

Austin's businesses and residents have some of the highest use of consumer-choice renewable energy of any US metro area. To satisfy that demand, the city's public utility, Austin Energy, has tapped into a diverse network of solar, wind and other forms of renewables.

Mayor Wynn has also pushed adoption of an emerging transportation technology, the plug-in hybrid electric vehicle. The idea is to drive demand so that the Big Three auto companies and other manufacturers will have a ready-made base of customers and thus will commit to mass production of these 100-mile-per-gallon wonders.

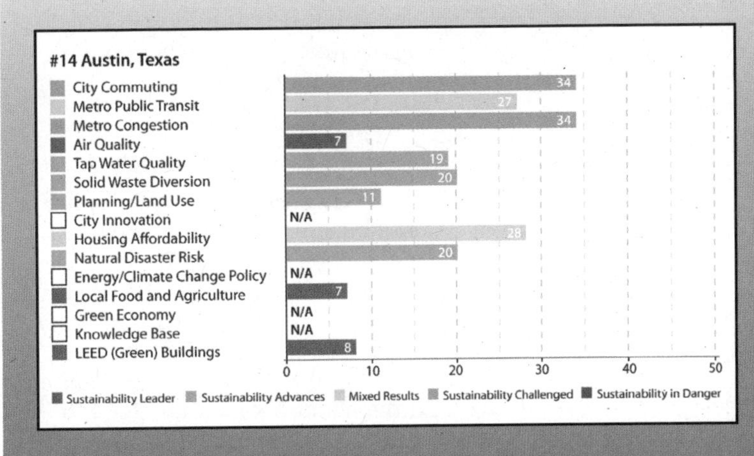

Given such a clear commitment to sustainability, why isn't Austin in the top ten of SustainLane's US City Rankings? Mainly because the city remains heavily car-dependent, with critical ramifications for congestion and overall economic health.

Healthy Living

Austin's air quality remains clean most of the time (#7), and tap water quality is above average (#19).

Parks are plentiful, taking up almost 14 percent of the city's land (#10). Austin's 206 parks, 12 sanctuaries for native plants and animals and 26 greenbelts offer an amazing diversity of recreation and native ecosystem preservation on fields and courts, along creek beds, and in canyons.

The local food system is thriving, too (#7). You can take advantage of ten farmers' markets, numerous community-supported agriculture providers, and high-profile community gardens and demonstration centers.

But Austin's Mayor Will Wynn is taking an active role in trying to reduce the city's dependence on fossil fuels with new technologies such as plug-in hybrids.

Getting Around

We'll cut right to it: Austin either has insufficient public transit or a population particularly inclined to drive. Capital Metro is the city's sole means of public transit, and it seems to be getting lonelier as time goes on. Public transit ridership fell from about 5 percent in 2000 to about 2 percent in 2004. Many Austin voters did try in 2000 to get light rail, but the measure lost by a narrow margin.

It's not that people are using other means of transport in Austin. Less than 3 percent walk or bike to work. Compare that to Washington, DC, a city of similar size in which more than 12 percent walk or bike to work. The vast majority of Austinites drive to work by themselves — about 79 percent in 2004.

As oil prices rise, car dependence is casting a shadow on the city's accomplishments — oil dependency is the part of the sustainability equation that is most likely to reach crisis mode. For the first time, Austin is on the verge of being noncompliant with the EPA's Clean Air Act. The city ranks #34 for congestion, #27 for metro public transportation ridership, and #34 for commute to work.

But Austin's Mayor Will Wynn is taking an active role in trying to reduce the city's dependence on fossil fuels with new technologies such as plug-in hybrids:

> How can we help tie the energy and transportation sectors together to really start to have a more holistic view of sustainability? ... A relatively simple answer is essentially taking existing hybrid technology vehicles and by dramatically expanding the battery capacity and then having the ability with a plug-in charger on the vehicle itself where folks would be able to simply plug their car in to a wall socket mostly overnight and get a charge with technology advancements it could represent fifty, seventy, maybe ninety miles of commuting the next day. The vast, vast majority of Americans commute less than twenty-five miles each day. So here's this opportunity to tie what has been this big massive transportation sector into this big massive energy sector and start to see what kind of efficiencies and synergies there can be.

Economic Factors

Because Austin did not respond to our survey, we were unable to officially rank the city in some categories related to economic development. That doesn't mean there isn't a lot going on. Austin is a recognized leader in the green economy, one of the few cities in our study that has a working public-private-academic clean tech incubator and numerous businesses focusing on renewable energy and green products and services.

Clean tech start-ups are thriving, developing everything from biofuels and advanced transportation to geothermal and fuel cells. One local company, MicroDynamo, is even investigating the storage of human-powered energy in batteries for small devices.

Austin's maturing green building industry is amassing impressive case histories, with the city ranking #8 in LEED buildings. Austin's Green Building Program juices the local economy with value-added products and services. For participating homeowners and businesses, Austin's green building programs are having a demonstrable effect on lowering energy and water use, cutting residents' long-term costs.

Austin skyline with solar panels. Austin is a leading city for renewable energy development.

City of Austin

Austin is very strong in green business and is highly appealing to cultural creatives, much like Portland, Denver and San Francisco.

Summary/Next Steps

Commuter or light rail, bus rapid transit, monorail? All of the above? Austin's biggest opportunity to rise in the rankings is to create public transit options. To convince voters in the next election, the Economic Development office could point out all the money that leaves Austin's local economy as all those drive-alone-everywhere citizens pay hundreds of dollars for gas each month.

Austin is very strong in green business and is highly appealing to cultural creatives, much like Portland, Denver and San Francisco. The difference is that these other three cities have, or are building, healthy public transit options to offer their business base. Potential employees considering moving to these other cities can put a check beside "ease of commuting on public transit to work," as can employers wanting to relocate knowledgeable workers. Austin will need to consider how sustainable its cultural creative growth can be considering its lagging public transit options.

15

Honolulu, Hawai'i

Almost Paradise

People know Honolulu, of course, for its location, location, location. The ocean acts as a giant thermostat, warming and moisturizing Arctic winds over thousands of miles. By the time that air gets to Hawaii, it's a balmy 78 degrees.

Though Honolulu's population is smallish, at about 375,000, in a single month just as many tourists can pass through the city. Honolulu is also an important transit hub, with a lot of global freight and military traffic.

The need for sustainability can be especially acute for island cities because of their partial reliance on faraway supplies and processing. Honolulu has made strides toward sustainability, but could benefit greatly from further efforts.

"Our pristine environment, from the mountains to the sea, has always been precious to our residents and visitors alike," said Honolulu Mayor Mufi Hannemann. "Whether it's waste-to-energy recycling, developing clean mass transit, or striving to be more energy-efficient, we've been taking the necessary steps to insure that our island home, with its many unique challenges, is cared for, following in the footsteps of the indigenous people who first called Honolulu home."

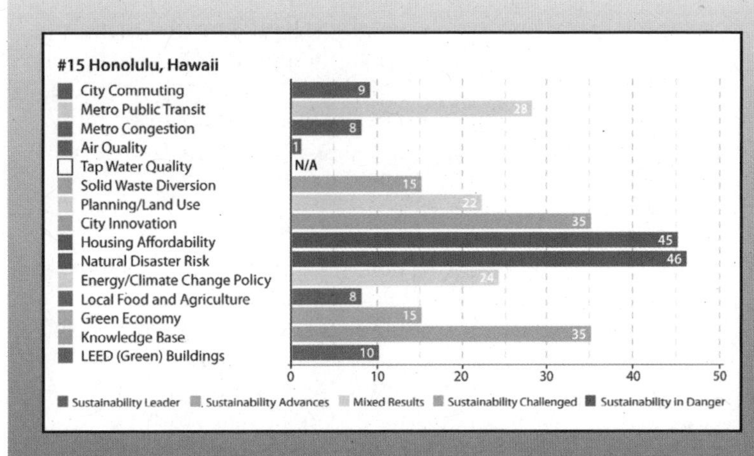

Healthy Living

Come to Honolulu for the air — the city ranks #1 in air quality due to its location and landscape. Breezes take pollutants out to sea, and clouds buoyed along by those winds beat against the mountaintops, bathing slopes and valleys in warm rain, which then filters down through volcanic rock to pool in deep aquifers. This water, pumped and cleaned by the city, meets all EPA guidelines for safe drinking (and tastes exceptionally pure), though we were not able to officially rank the city's water quality, as it was not available in Environmental

Working Group's tap water quality database.

Honolulu has more farmers' markets per capita than any of the other cities we studied. Residents and visitors enjoy a large number of markets for fresh, island-grown produce sourced from local farmers' and fishers. A city-managed project called the People's Open Market runs 25 market sites, drawing a million shoppers every year. For more upscale fare, the weekly farmers' market held in the parking lot of the Kapiolani Community College features organic greens, aqua-farmed shrimp, aged honey, and heirloom tomatoes.

Getting Around

The layout of Honolulu is linear and would benefit from a rail system. About 10 percent of the city's commuters do ride public transit to work, putting the city at #13. As is usually the case in US cities, most commuters in Honolulu drive alone (about 62 percent), and regularly complain about traffic.

Honolulu, already blessed with so much, could show us how to maximize nature's gifts — and truly shine as a sustainability leader.

At the same time, the island metropolis is slightly ahead of the curve in terms of people cycling to work, probably because it's a joy to be outside. Honolulu also enjoys the first and largest vanpooling company in the US, and more people reportedly rideshare here than anywhere else in the country.

Biodiesel is catching on in the islands. Honolulu drivers can pump the cleaner fuel thanks to businesses like Pacific Biodiesel, which has a plant in the city and ambitions to run the state's truck and marine fleet on biodiesel.

Economic Factors

The Natural Energy Laboratory of Hawaii Authority hosts many businesses doing proof-of-concept research in aquaculture. Plankton, shrimp, abalone, clams, coral, seaweed, lobsters and a variety of fish are being harvested there rather than at natural fisheries. Successes in aquaculture can only bolster Hawaii's already commendable steps toward local food production. Many similar endeavors are also underway.

Honolulu ranks #10 in LEED buildings per capita, though the city does not have any green building incentive programs. With proper incentives, the city could become a national leader in green building.

Summary/Next Steps

Honolulu is doing well compared to other US cities, and in certain areas it deserves praise and emulation. In terms of energy, transportation and overall sustainability planning, however, Honolulu doesn't distinguish itself from the pack. It has an opportunity to wrangle more energy from its breezy and sunlit clime. Almost 80 percent of the city's electricity comes from the combustion of oil, and the city has virtually no renewables in its total energy mix. Honolulu, already blessed with so much, could show us how to maximize nature's gifts — and truly shine as a sustainability leader.

16

Milwaukee, Wisconsin

From Beer to Biomass

When it comes to sustainability, Wisconsin's largest city often gets overshadowed by Madison, which, aside from already having a University of Wisconsin campus, has a reputation for being forward-thinking and eco-friendly. But Milwaukee has stately Lake Michigan, a major public transportation system with ridership of 10 percent of the city's commuters, low sprawl and great potential for urban redevelopment.

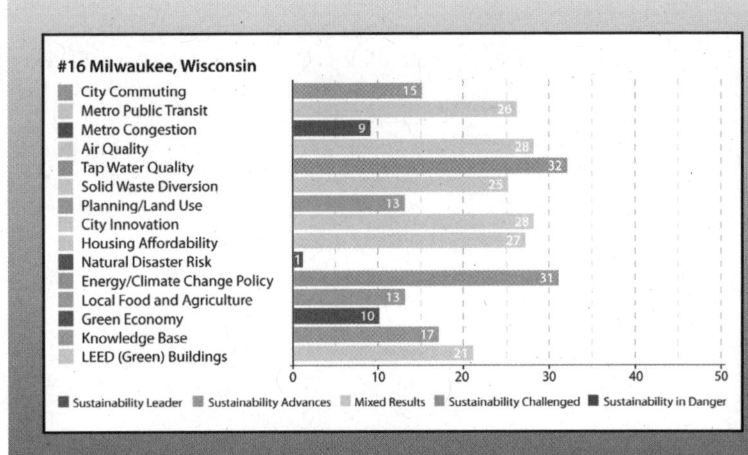

Milwaukee is also taking advantage of its easy access to lake- and river-front based recreation, an asset that was surprisingly neglected until the 1990s. Lake Michigan has since been reimagined with parks and museums, and the Milwaukee River has been gussied up with walkways, benches and hangout spots for pedestrians and cyclists. You can cruise the waterways in a kayak or canoe, stopping along the way at a small business to browse books, eat lunch or have a beer.

Beer, yes — the once largely Germanic city has been home to the headquarters of Miller, Schlitz and Pabst, as well as countless brands that have gone the way of the dodo (Blatz, anyone?). Still flavored by its German immigrant heritage, Milwaukee has assumed much greater diversity, with substantial populations of African, Asian, Italian, Polish and Arab Americans.

Healthy Living

Quality-of-life indicators are mixed, such as air quality (#28) and tap water quality (#32). Lake Michigan sure looks pretty, but for drinking purposes it's less appealing — the city's tap water has 24 contaminants, 4 of which surpass the EPA's recommended limit. Despite such concerns, Milwaukee's slower pace, decent walkability and uncongested roads (#9) make it feel healthier than many other cities, and it

Milwaukee has maintained its old-fashioned charm, while embracing New Urbanist redevelopment approaches that encourage walk-ability, mixed-use development, and downtown density.

devotes 9.8 percent of city acreage to parks (#19). The plans for Erie Street Plaza take into consideration the principles of sustainability by restoring a once-contaminated brownfield with native plants and a bamboo grove while keeping stormwater onsite and further beautifying the revitalized waterfront.

Wisconsin's love of sausage, cheese and bratwurst doesn't exactly conjure up the picture of health. But the city has access to networks of smaller farms and orchards; cherries and apples in particular thrive in the northerly climate. Milwaukee has almost 50 community gardens and 8 farmers' markets, which puts it at #13 in the nation for local food and agriculture.

Getting Around

Public transportation is alive and kicking in Milwaukee, with about 10 percent riding it to work everyday. Another 10 percent or so commute via carpool, and almost 5 percent walk or bike to work. That leaves about 73 percent who drive alone every day to get to work, perhaps encouraged by the lack of traffic congestion. But even without congestion, that drive-alone rate will sap money out of the local economy and pollute at a much greater rate than in cities that are less dependent on autos.

Economic Factors

Green buildings are on the rise throughout the city, with 4 LEED Registered and 3 LEED Certified structures, placing Milwaukee #21 in LEED buildings per capita. The city gets 2 percent of its energy from renewable resources, including wind and biomass. In 2006, Milwaukee's City Hall got 10 percent of its energy from renewable sources and Mayor Tom Barrett has directed city departments to reduce energy use by 10 percent, in part through vending machine misers that shut off the machines during non-business hours.

Housing affordability ranks a mediocre #27. Average housing prices are just under $112,000, but the average income is only $31,000.

Summary/Next Steps

A new Milwaukee Green Team advisory committee appointed by Mayor Barrett appears to be making headway on coordinating more action in the area of sustainability planning and management. The team consists of business leaders, academics and government and community organization representatives. As part of their recommendations, the city and Mayor Barrett are working with the nonpartisan Apollo Alliance to jump-start clean-tech industry efforts recommended by the Green Team. Additionally, in 2006, the mayor appointed a sustainability department director and support staff.

Milwaukee has maintained its old-fashioned charm, while embracing New Urbanist redevelopment approaches that encourage walk-ability, mixed-use development, and downtown density. With conscious efforts to fold sustainability planning and design into the mix, Milwaukee could become the second city on Lake Michigan to make a name for itself with such innovative approaches.

17

San Diego, California

An Emerging Leader?

What's not to like? Warm days cooled by ocean breezes, easy access to beaches and parks, and a revitalized downtown make for good living. Behind this idyllic setting, San Diego does have opportunities to become more sustainable — by creating markets for local food, improving its tap water quality, enhancing public transit and addressing its high cost of living. Fortunately, San Diego shows evidence of a growing awareness of green building, renewable energy sources, and strategies to reduce sprawl.

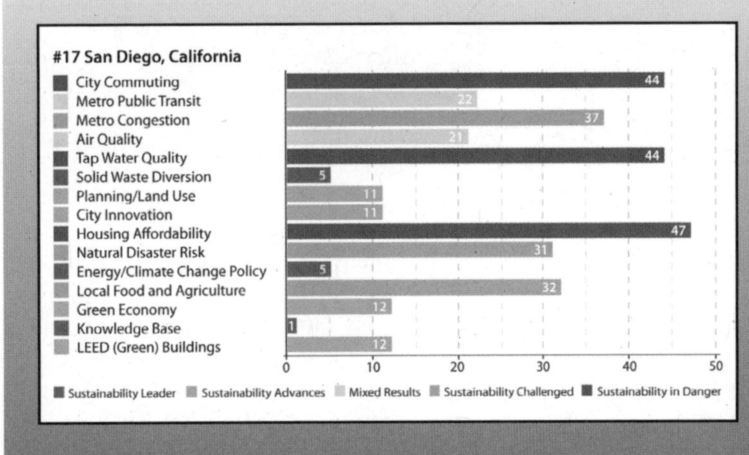

Healthy Living

San Diego gets its water from the Colorado River, 1,500 miles away, and from Northern California, 600 miles away. An enormous amount of non-renewable energy is used to get this water to the tap. And partially because of the water's epic journey past freeways and industry through open-air canals, San Diego tap water (#44) has 27 contaminants, with 5 over the recommended threshold.

San Diego can boast about its parks (#4 nationally) and outdoor recreation opportunities. A trip to Balboa Park lets you enjoy wide-open spaces with gardens, fountains and museums. There are also world-renowned theaters, shopping and restaurants, particularly in the city's Gaslamp Quarter.

There are only 5 farmers' markets in San Diego for a population over 1 million — a surprisingly low rate for a city so well situated near agricultural areas. It's unfortunate that the abundant produce from the farmers' markets in Los Angeles doesn't make its way down to San Diego, only two hours away. None of the San Diego farmers' markets accepts food stamps. A lack of community gardens contributes to the city's overall local food/agriculture ranking of #32.

Getting Around

Whether you're a resident or a tourist, you're most likely to use a car to get around San Diego. Very few people use public transit, walk or bike because the metropolitan area is so spread out and criss-crossed with highways. Despite warm weather and a physically fit population, 81 percent of San Diegans drive alone to work.

Less than 3 percent of the population uses public transit. Alternatives to the car do exist — buses and a trolley-style light rail developed in 1981 — but locals report that these systems are not convenient commuting options. There are many network routes for recreational bicycle travel, especially along the beach. As with Los Angeles, though, citywide utilitarian cycling alternatives are limited and very few people bike to work (less than 1 percent).

Overall, San Diego ranks #44 in commute to work, #22 in public transportation, and #37 for congestion — very poor scores for a city of some 1.2 million people.

Economic Factors

San Diego's economy is thriving. Booming biotech and electronics industries help keep unemployment very low.

San Diego's economy is thriving. Booming biotech and electronics industries help keep unemployment very low. The city government plays a significant role in guaranteeing more sustainable development approaches.

Downtown San Diego has been enjoying urban renewal. A smart growth scheme led by the city and local residents aims to increase density downtown as the population increases to a projected three times the present number. Plans emphasize multi-use projects that will double employment and offer more housing downtown. There are also incentives to build along the trolley routes, and plans for more parks, affordable housing and historic preservation projects. Critics of the scheme worry about traffic congestion and parking shortages, but in a sprawling, car-dependent city, it's a step toward a sustainable downtown.

Many green buildings are being planned in San Diego, with 22 LEED Registered buildings and four already certified (#12). All city construction must meet a minimum of LEED Silver certification, which means projects include everything from waterless urinals, day lighting, renewable energy, water-saving xeriscape plantings, and more.

California's rigid standards for recycling and waste diversion have helped San Diego accomplish a waste diversion rate of 53 percent (#5), and some neighborhoods have implemented a green waste program. The city also reports that 8 percent of its energy mix comes from renewable energy. That rate could increase even more if the city made better use of its abundant sunshine; many of the current renewable sources are hooked into the grid at a great distance from the city.

While San Diego is thriving economically, it is also one of the most expensive places to live in the country, ranking #47 in affordability.

Less vulnerable to major earthquakes than nearby Los Angeles, San Diego ranks #31 in natural disaster risk. The city is at risk for flooding and even tsunamis, and was destroyed in its early years by a moderate earthquake.

Summary/Next Steps

Economically, San Diego is thriving, with low unemployment, economic innovation, and a revitalized urban core. In many ways, both residents and city government are putting their money where their mouth is. Residents benefit from economic growth that has incorporated green building and businesses that cater to fitness. San Diego is definitely a leader in the emerging economic realm of sustainability.

There remain some significant opportunities, however. Despite its coastal location, favorable climate, and abundant parks, San Diego is not doing as well in terms of overall quality of life. It has poor water quality and needs improved access to local food. And if the city wants to remain economically competitive as it redevelops its city center, it needs to invest in public transportation so that using it becomes an everyday experience for more residents.

Wikipedia / CreativeCommons 2.5

One America Plaza, Seaport Village in downtown San Diego.

18

Kansas City, Missouri

Laying the Groundwork

Kansas City, Missouri might be known for its jazz history, stride piano and barbecue sauce, but it's also making strides in city sustainability. At the junction of the Kansas and Missouri rivers, the city is surrounded by a relatively flat landscape with a smattering of rolling hills. However, the combination of a lack of real natural boundaries and the growing popularity of the automobile made typical post–World War II sprawl almost inevitable.

As the city expanded outward, the thriving downtown began to decline. The automobile reigned supreme and money was funneled into building roads. Kansas City now has more miles of freeway per person than any other city in the nation, according to the local transit advocacy group Smart Moves.

While sprawl continues and most residents remain committed to auto travel, leading indicators point toward a more sustainable future for Kansas City. Without a champion for sustainability, such as a mayor or city manager, or even a sustainability plan, the city's sustainability efforts have been piecemeal until recently. However, progress is being made in some very innovative areas. Mayor Kay Barnes' 2006 addition of an Environmental Department, increased plans for public transit, green building, community gardens and pristine water quality are just a few examples.

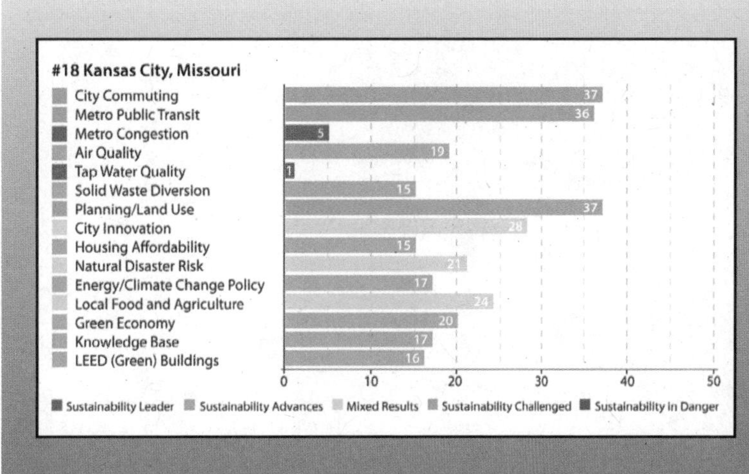

Healthy Living

Kansas City's water quality ranks #1 of all the cities in our study, with no contaminants detected or pollutants over EPA-designated levels. The source, the Missouri River, is polluted before being transformed in state-of-the-art treatment plants. Once it leaves the tap, the water is so good, in fact, that in 1998 the city began to bottle and sell it. City

One of Kansas City, Missouri's 10,000 Rain Gardens collects rainwater, then cleans and filters the water with native plants.

Fountains Premium Bottled Water is the top-selling municipally owned bottled water in the Midwest.

That doesn't mean Kansas City is resting on its laurels. The truly innovative 10,000 Rain Gardens initiative calls on citizens, corporations, nonprofits and city government to voluntarily reduce runoff that pollutes the waterways by creating "rain gardens" — shallow depressions designed to collect rain so that plants and bacteria can clean the water as it enters the ground. One stormwater specialist calls these rain gardens "truly sustainable in a way that our current system is not." The rain gardens clean the water, prevent contamination and recharge water into a depleting water source. And they involve the entire community in the process.

LYNN HINKLE, ASTRA COMMUNICATIONS, KANSAS CITY, MO

Officially, Kansas City has two community food gardens. Kansas City Community Gardens is a non-profit dedicated to improving quality of life in low-income households and for the community by helping people grow their own fruits and vegetables. The gardens are so popular that reservations are needed. In fact, overflow has initiated gardens in backyards, churches, vacant lots and community centers. (The organization helps with those gardens as well.)

You can also find local produce at the big outdoor City Market each Sunday. But, despite the abundance of locally grown food vendors and the obvious interest in purchasing their goods, the city has only three farmers' markets. Overall, Kansas City ranks #24 in local food and agriculture.

Swope Park is an inner-city park that covers over one thousand acres and has a lake, an amphitheater and sporting activities. Despite this and other parks, parkways and gardens, the total amount of city land devoted to parks places Kansas City near the middle of our rankings at #26.

Getting Around

More than 80 percent of Kansas City residents commute to work in their car alone. There are no carshare or carpool programs, and very few people commute via bicycle or walking. Only 3.9 percent of residents take public transportation to work.

Those bleak statistics might be changing, however. In 2003, voters approved a city sales tax increase to fund a bus system expansion and upgrade; the new bus system, MAX, began in 2005. Smart Moves, a joint initiative of the Mid America Regional Council, Kansas City Area Transit Authority, and other regional transit entities, encourages the connection of the suburbs to each other and to downtown using an innovative bus system.

The city has made a commitment to a less-polluting vehicle fleet that doesn't depend solely on foreign oil. Almost 45 percent of its city fleet vehicles use alternative fuel, one of the highest rates among the 50 largest US cities.

Economic Factors

After years of neglect, downtown Kansas City is coming alive again. A planned entertainment district, sports arena and expanding real estate development converting vacant commercial buildings to loft-style housing are good first steps. New transit plans will ensure better public transportation downtown. Both the government and residents seem to have a renewed commitment to the city's core, but the new plans do not yet incorporate any type of significant sustainable elements for the downtown plan.

Kansas City is emerging as a leader in green building, ranking #16. All new city buildings in a Kansas City are now required to meet LEED Silver certification. Kansas City is also participating in a LEED for Existing Buildings pilot program for its City Hall. The Kansas City Science Center, which is LEED Gold-Certified, features a water recovery system that captures and filters rainwater.

Although the city doesn't offer residential or commercial green

Kansas City is emerging as a leader in green building, ranking #16. All new city buildings in a Kansas City are now required to meet LEED Silver certification.

From rain gardens to internationally recognized green building projects, Kansas City has no shortage of sustainability-related programs and organizations.

building incentives, the Homebuilders Association of Greater Kansas City has a voluntary green building program based on all four levels of LEED certification. The program demonstrates community awareness and interest in green building, featuring at least six green homebuilders within the city.

Summary/Next Steps

From rain gardens to internationally recognized green building projects, Kansas City has no shortage of sustainability-related programs and organizations. Hopefully, the city's addition of an Environmental Department in 2006 will provide an overall sustainability framework. The city still has a very high rate of automobile use, no renewables in its energy mix, a limited bus system, no green business guide and limited access to a locally produced food supply. By integrating the various efforts into a broader, more systemic approach to sustainability, the city will be better able to create long-term solutions to its current and future challenges.

19

Albuquerque, New Mexico

Making a U-Turn

Until now, if you lived in or visited Albuquerque, you needed a car for everything. Like many Western cities after WWII, Albuquerque was developed with the open road in mind. Miles and miles of asphalt link retailers, office space, residential areas and schools.

Sixty years later, that's beginning to change, in part because of a forward-thinking mayor, Martin Chavez. The "Chavez Era" has brought sustainability policies and pro-business economic development to the same table. As you make your way through the streets now, you may notice an increase in public transportation, better linkages between neighborhoods, more green building projects, and a large fleet of green city vehicles.

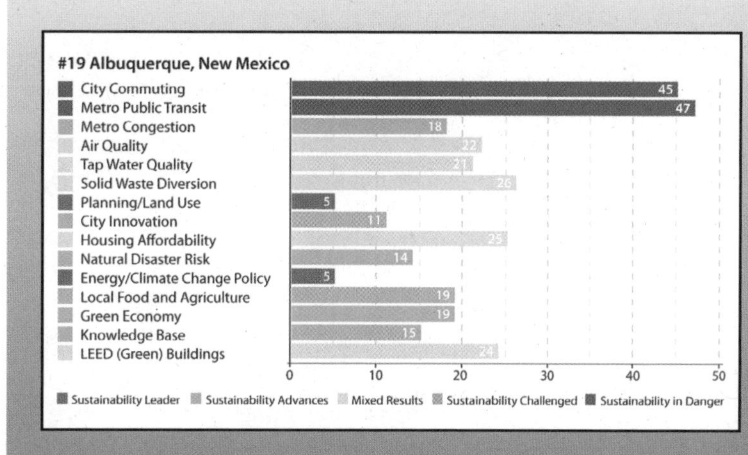

Healthy Living

Albuquerque offers an abundance of community gardens, farmers' markets and public parks. Four farmers' markets dispersed throughout the city provide a variety of locally produced food.

If you want to grow your own food or learn how others are doing it, there are three community gardens and three more are in the planning phase — and the Alley Garden Project aspires to create even more. One of the largest gardens, Rio Grande Community Farm, demonstrates the "Triple Bottom Line" principles of sustainability — economy, ecology and community — with 90 acres for commercial heirloom crops, 38 acres for bird migration and other wildlife, and 10 acres for individual gardeners. In a city blessed with abundant sunshine, parks are a viable asset, and 15.4 percent of city land is devoted to them.

Do consider getting a water filter if you're living in Albuquerque: Water (#21) and air quality (#22) are just slightly above average.

Getting Around

Albuquerque is among the worst in local transportation performance in our study, ranking #47 for regional public transportation and #45 for more sustainable city commute practices (public transit, biking, walking or carpooling). While public transit ridership has risen the past two years, according to 2004 data it was still around only 2 percent of all transportation, while biking and walking for commuting were virtually nonexistent. Almost all residents commute to work in their cars alone. To change this, Mayor Chavez has committed to giving the residents more options. One new alternative is Rapid Ride, an express trolley that services shopping, entertainment and dining. It's even equipped with wireless access and books for children. Several other public transit alternatives are in the implementation phase, including light rail. Carshare and carpool programs are offered, though the most recent numbers indicate that these are not yet heavily used alternatives.

The mayor has also committed to a 100 percent green city fleet. Presently 42 percent of the city's vehicles run on alternative fuel, making Albuquerque a national leader in that category.

Economic Factors

The mayor has a vested interest in creating an economic base that supports sustainability. Although there are presently no green building incentives, the mayor has committed to green building standards for official city building construction. The city has plans to extend those standards to both residential and commercial building. Albuquerque ranks #25 in housing affordability, with an average housing price of $140,000.

Unfortunately, none of the city's energy mix currently utilizes renewable energy, though the city is targeting 15 percent to 25 percent renewables for city buildings over the next few years. Albuquerque's Million Solar Roofs program, for instance, facilitates thermal and PV solar systems for public buildings. In 2006, the city passed a resolution earmarking $1 million for future

WIKIPEDIA: "RAPID RIDE"

Rapid Ride, the city's new hybrid-diesel Bus Rapid Transit and possible harbinger of a light rail future.

solar business development incentives and tax credits.

Summary/Next Steps

While Albuquerque ranks low in categories related to public transit, an inspired mayor has instituted several programs to make the city more sustainable. Increased public transportation, green building incentives, and a sizable green fleet are an excellent start. A growing local food supply, a local water source (the Rio Grande), affordability, and a significant amount of parkland indicate that Albuquerque has the infrastructure to make sustainable living in the desert a reality.

The city could make further strides by boosting public transit options and awareness; creating a more dense, walkable city center; and offering tangible incentives to encourage green building projects and emerging clean tech economies. The Rio Grande, which ran completely dry during the drought of 1996, needs to be carefully managed and protected throughout its watershed.

Unlike many other cities, Albuquerque recognizes its limitations toward a sustainable future and has instituted policies and programs to begin changing. As the city scales up its efforts, they are likely to take hold and become part of the city's everyday way of doing things.

WIKIPEDIA / GNU FDL1.2

Albuquerque's downtown car dependence is a situation city leaders are trying to overcome.

Tucson, Arizona

Becoming Sustainable in the Sun Belt

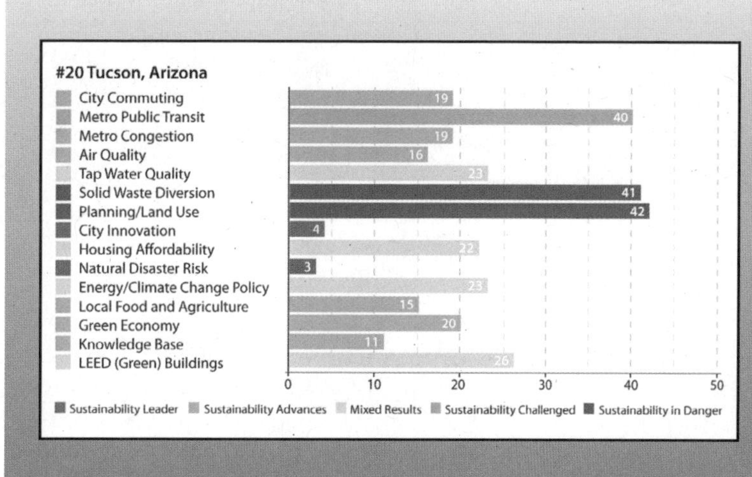

More people keep coming to Tucson either as new residents, tourists or students at the University of Arizona. If you decide to become one of those newcomers, you'll find that Tucson, though still affordable, offers a high quality of life. You'll get sunny skies practically 365 days a year, a vibrant arts community, and nearby wilderness recreational activities including hiking, biking, rock climbing and skiing on Mt. Lemmon. However, the city's burgeoning population has formed a tenuous relationship with the desert's fragile ecosystem, as is symbolized by the diminishing Santa Cruz River.

Healthy Living

Air quality is generally good, ranking #16, but be careful about what you put in your water bottle. Tucson's tap water quality (#23) isn't terrible, but it isn't great, either, with 27 contaminants, including 2 that are over the EPA's recommended limit. The city is working to address its water quality by collaborating with the National Science Foundation Water Quality Center to research the safety, health and aesthetics of water quality.

It's easy to find a farmers' market in Tucson that will satisfy your need for high-quality food. Ranging from semi-tropical and tropical fruits and vegetables to grass-fed beef, local food products are surprisingly diverse considering Tucson's desert location. Many inspired neighborhoods have instituted community gardens, providing a place for neighbors to gather and grow their own food and to learn how to start their own gardens.

Getting Around

You won't have trouble finding parking in Tucson; most buildings don't exceed three stories and the city has in the past required extensive parking, encouraging automotive use — policies that have supported a tendency toward sprawl. It comes as no surprise that 73 percent of the population drives alone to work.

Unlike those in higher-density US cities, people in Tucson are not in the habit of using public transit, with only 3.7 percent riding the bus to work. With federal funding cuts, riding transit has become more of a hassle as buses come less frequently and trips require several transfers. On the brighter side, 14 percent of the population carpools to work.

Tucsonans have 325 miles of bike lanes, 100 signed bike routes, and 55 miles of shared (bike and pedestrian) paths, making it easy to take advantage of year-round sun. No wonder Tucson ranks #3 in bike commuting, with 2 percent of its population pedaling to work.

Tucson has developed green building incentives for residential and commercial building and had 8 registered LEED buildings as of early 2006.

Economic Factors

In order to guarantee a more sustainable economic base, the city has developed green building incentives for residential and commercial building and had 8 registered LEED buildings as of early 2006. Combined with the abundant local food, these two factors contribute to an above-average green local economy. The city does rank low for its use of renewable energy, however, with 95 percent of the power supplied by coal and only 1 percent by renewables.

Tucson is close to the middle of the pack in terms of affordability (#22), with relatively low median housing prices and a living wage.

Summary/Next Steps

Tucson has many innovative projects in the pipeline or already up and running, including a "one-stop shop" landfill program that incorporates diverse options for recycling, waste disposal and an education facility.

Tucson is ahead of many other Sun Belt cities because it has recognized the necessity for sustainability planning in its future road map. A new city manager and an active city council have placed sustainability at the forefront of their agenda, giving the office of environmental affairs more authority and funding.

This hasn't stemmed car-dependent development, but city incentives to limit sprawl and get people out of their cars are a good first step. Waste diversion, at 14 percent, is low compared to that of other cities, but the one-stop-shop landfill could improve that rate through public awareness and ease of use. Finally, in a city where solar is such a viable alternative, the existing rate of only 1 percent alternative energy use is low, though the sunny city is working with solar-energy groups to increase the use of solar power.

21

San Antonio, Texas

Building on a Broad Range of Strengths

San Antonio is known as Military City due to its four military installations and the many military retirees who stay in town. Nestled in rolling hills, it features warm winters and a lush green walkway called the River Walk (or *Paseo Del Rio*) in the heart of downtown. As the oldest city in Texas, it also offers historic attractions, including four Spanish Missions and The Alamo. Some 20 million visitors take in the sights annually — coming as tourists, for conventions, or on military assignment. The Air Force conducts basic training in San Antonio, and both the Army and Air Force medical schools are here; the Army's is the largest healthcare training facility in the world.

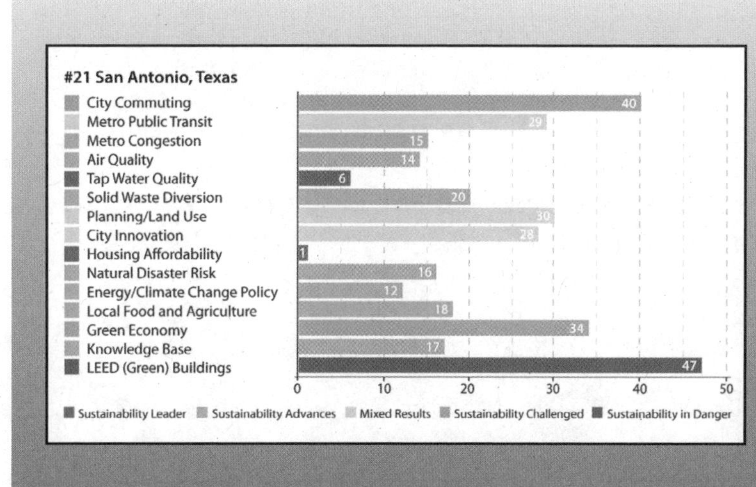

Healthy Living

San Antonio ranks #18 in local food and agriculture, and parks cover 6.3 percent of its area. Air quality in San Antonio is relatively good (#14).

San Antonio sits on one of the most prolific artesian aquifers in the world, and its water quality is ranked #6 in our study. However, the aquifer is sensitive to overuse; the San Antonio Water System declared 2006 levels to be very low, a prelude to summer drought restrictions. No surface water system or any other alternative system has ever been built. As the population continues to grow in San Antonio, the city faces a serious question about how to protect the groundwater supply that, centuries ago, allowed Spanish missionaries to establish a stronghold next to the vast Chihuahuan Desert.

Getting Around

San Antonio is part of the I-35 corridor, the most significant blacktop in Texas. No other state exports as much as Texas, and I-35 conveys freight trucks to Canada and Mexico. Commuters use the highway as well as truckers, so traffic in outlying areas is bad and getting worse. Attempts at developing public transit, including light rail, haven't been very successful. About 2 percent of commuters use existing public transportation. Nearly 80 percent of San Antonians drive to work alone.

Nevertheless, San Antonio gets a good mark for traffic congestion within the city, ranking #15. Congestion is kept under control in part by highway management systems that monitor traffic flow with cameras and pressure strips, and then automatically coordinate traffic lights throughout the urban grid accordingly. These "smart highways" report congestion on large electronic billboards along the highway. San Antonio, an early adopter of this technology, serves as a case study example for other cities considering it.

Economic Factors

San Antonio has shown strong initiative in the use of renewable energy and in greenhouse gas emission tracking; the city ranks #12 in this category. About 2.5 percent of the city's power comes from wind

The River Walk in San Antonio.

COURTESY SACVB/AL RENDON

energy. Texas is ranked second nationwide in terms of wind energy potential, with the panhandle and West Texas Mountains providing sufficient wind to keep windmills spinning. A cluster of huge wind generators in West Texas called Desert Sky is being tapped by the power utility in San Antonio to give subscribers the option to buy wind power. On a smaller scale, natural gas produced by rotting waste is also being used to supplement the city's grid.

These efforts to diversify San Antonio's energy infrastructure are bolstered by educational and outreach programs by local nonprofits such as Solar San Antonio. Another nonprofit, the Metropolitan Partnership for Energy, runs outreach programs such as Build San Antonio Green, which spreads the word on green residential construction among builders and homeowners. Though the city lags behind most others in green building (#47), it has 5 LEED buildings registered and due to be built.

A living wage and low housing costs help make San Antonio the most affordable city in our study. The median home price is $88,000 and the median monthly rent for apartments is $550, both well below the national average.

Summary/Next Steps

San Antonio's population has grown significantly over the last two decades, which could present challenges down the road. While the city's highway management system has limited congestion, offering public transportation options that get people out of their cars would help it support its growing population — a strong argument in favor of developing light rail.

The city's sustainability planning might benefit as well from the military. Starting in 2006, all Army installations must comply with environmental benchmarks. The Army already has its own green building certification standard, based on LEED, called Sustainable Project Rating Tool (SPiRiT). By 2009, the Army aims to be entirely compliant with ISO 14000, a strict international standard for implementing environmental management systems. The other military branches are expected to follow suit. Taking a cue from its military installations, the city has an opportunity to come up with a more focused sustainability plan that can move it into a leadership position.

Texas is ranked second nationwide in terms of wind energy potential, with the panhandle and West Texas Mountains providing sufficient wind to keep windmills spinning.

22

Phoenix, Arizona

Something New Under the Sun

Phoenix has a reputation as a retirement community with a relaxing desert environment, abundant sunshine and lots of golf courses — and until recently, it was pretty much just that. In 1950, there were only 105,000 people living within the city limits and less than half the streets were paved. Now, Phoenix is the fifth-largest city in the United States.

Because Phoenix is such a new city and has grown so fast, it is markedly different from other large US cities. Phoenicians resisted growth by trying to preserve a small-town feel (it wasn't until the 1980s that the city surrendered to a highway system). Its residents are passionate about preserving wide-open landscape views, so growth has been channeled into low-density sprawl.

Climate is one of Phoenix's defining features. In the Navajo language, Phoenix is called *Hoozdo*, or "the place is hot." The summer temperature exceeds 100 degrees an average of 89 days of the year, with a record high of 122 degrees in 1990. Phoenix lies in a valley in the heart of the Sonoran Desert. Winters are mild and sunny with huge temperature fluctuations. Daytime temperatures might reach 70 degrees while nighttime temperatures can plummet to 30 degrees.

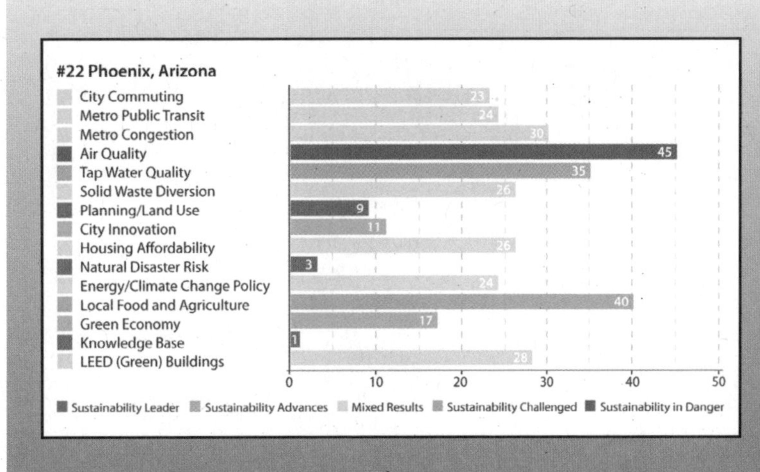

Healthy Living

Water is always a topic of conversation in an urban desert environment. Phoenix is one of the few desert cities with a local water supply. The Salt River, its water source, runs through the city. Its riverbed is normally dry, except during a flood, when one of the four dams upriver releases water. The tap water contains 27 contaminants, including 4 over the recommended legal limit (#35); residents might want to consider a water filter for their tap.

Urban parks have become a priority for the city. Residents and tourists can explore what is claimed to be the largest metropolitan park in the world, South Mountain Park. More parkland is on the way: In 1999, voters agreed to preserve 15,000 acres of land for 9 regional parks.

Phoenix is surrounded by farming communities that provide a wide variety of local produce, but residents can get it at only 6 farmers' markets (ranking #34), which is not very many for a city of over a million people. There are four community gardens in Phoenix.

In 1999, voters agreed to preserve 15,000 acres of land for 9 regional parks.

Getting Around

In its early days, Phoenix was a small desert town with gorgeous views and cheap land all around. Until recently, there was no highway system or extensive public transit. But all that's changing, as Phoenicians seek alternatives to auto travel. After many failed votes, voters approved the Phoenix Light Rail System in 2000. A 20-mile starter line was planned to open in 2006, with the entire line set to go full throttle by 2008, which should help open up possibilities for those beyond the 3 percent of the population who ride public transport to work every day. Light rail would also boost commuter ridership into a respectable range — it is projected to carry 3,000 to 5,000 passengers per hour during peak hours when it opens in late 2008, and could be a viable alternative to driving.

Economic Factors

As in many of the US cities in this study, Phoenix is only starting to address sustainability as part of its government planning. Phoenix does not have green building incentives for commercial or residential building projects. It does, however, have a growing number of LEED Certified green buildings (#28). About 1 percent of the city's energy mix uses renewable energy resources. In a city that boasts over 300 days of sun annually, solar energy installations could be a local economic development engine.

Summary/Next Steps

Due to its rapid growth, Phoenix is an adolescent compared to most other large US cities. As a result, the city faces challenges that many other large cities addressed long ago, though residents and government alike are beginning to address these issues. The introduction of light rail, expansion of urban parks and interest in LEED certified buildings are a good start. Another opportunity the city might consider would be to create incentives for urban infill projects and planning for public transit and pedestrian-friendly environments. The US Green Building Council's LEED for Neighborhood Developments, or LEED-ND, would be a great model for the city to use as a guideline.

23

San Jose, California

High Tech Hub Makes Strides

With 6,600 technology companies employing more than 250,000 highly skilled and highly educated workers, it's not surprising that residents of San Jose pull down the highest median income of any US city with more than 300,000 people. Less well known is that the city has had the lowest crime rate for three years running, and recycles more waste — a whopping 62 percent — than any of the cities we ranked outside of California.

There are downsides to this creative class economy, such as the gain and loss of nearly 200,000 jobs during the dot-com boom and bust, and a housing market in which homes cost more than triple the national average. San Jose's leaders have responded to these and other concerns with strategic economic planning in order to ensure San Jose's ongoing preeminence in the technology industry.

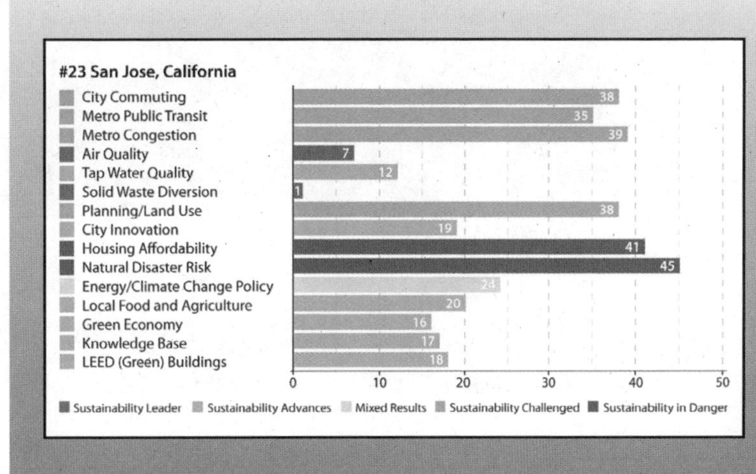

Healthy Living

The city's air ranks #7 despite the number of cars on the road and sprawling development, and the water is pretty clean at #12. The city also offers a newly revitalized, pedestrian-friendly downtown to relax in, but only 3.4 percent of city land is devoted to parks — the fourth-lowest percentage in our study.

The city has 19 community gardens, and an above-average ranking of #20 in local food, which remains lower than one might expect in light of its rich agricultural history.

San Jose is tied for first in waste diversion, but that's come partly by shifting responsibility for electronic waste control to developing countries. In US landfills, discarded computer cathode ray tubes and other electronics comprise a main source of hazardous waste contamination. Hewlett-Packard has been a leader in responsible e-waste practices,

COURTESY SAN JOSE CONVENTION & VISITORS BUREAU

Aerial view of Highway 87 as it passes through San Jose.

sponsoring take-back programs; hopefully more electronics makers will follow suit.

Getting Around

Despite traffic congestion (#39 nationally), more than 80 percent of San Jose residents drive alone to work. The city offers "ecopasses" to city employees that allow free rides on both the bus and light rail system, and all public transit vehicles have bicycle racks. Yet only 2 percent of residents ride public transit or walk to work, and less than 1 percent bike to work, despite the city's efforts to educate drivers, pedestrians and cyclists about sharing the streets through its Street Smarts program.

Economic Factors

Over the last several decades, the city's economy has grown rapidly and steadily, and its population has grown along with it — it's now the 10th largest US city. That growth hasn't left San Jose without challenges. Anti-sprawl measures have created a shortage of land for new housing, which has helped raise median home prices, severely affecting lower- and moderate-income residents.

A living wage ordinance helps city employees make ends meet, and the Teacher Homebuyer Program is an innovative program that has brought home ownership within reach of more than 428 teachers since 1999. Over the last several years, the city has also built several hundred affordable housing units, including a mixed-use housing development downtown.

The city has a variety of other initiatives to promote sustainable business, including a Green Business certification program, Environmentally Preferable Purchasing policies, and plans to install five renewable energy systems by 2008.

Summary/Next Steps

San Jose is among the cities best situated to promote — and reap the benefits of — a transition to a greener economy. Its educated, tech-savvy population and its proximity to venture capital make it one of the nation's leading incubation clusters for clean-tech start-ups. However, for the city to become a true leader in sustainability requires more than the ability to grow an industry — it requires sustainable behavior such as creating more affordable housing options for local residents, ensuring access to local food, and building in ways that reduce sprawl and traffic congestion.

At #23 overall, San Jose is beginning to address sustainability issues through its Environmental Services Department and its General Plan. Efforts to date include incorporating LEED building standards, promoting higher density and mixed-use neighborhood development, and revitalizing downtown. These represent a promising start.

San Jose could take a bigger step forward by offering commercial and residential incentives for green building and, taking a page from San Francisco's book, creating a greenhouse gas inventory to establish a baseline for reducing carbon emissions. It could also put more energy behind creating local food resources and encourage Silicon Valley technology businesses to institute responsible product-lifecycle stewardship programs, which would have repercussions for healthy living not just in the United States, but around the world.

San Jose is among the cities best situated to promote — and reap the benefits of — a transition to a greener economy.

24

Dallas, Texas

Taking the Bull by the Horns

Dallas is the glittering jewel in the crown of what's known locally as the Dallas-Arlington-Fort Worth Metroplex. The largest of the three cities, Dallas prides itself on being the hippest and most sophisticated city in North Texas. It has the best restaurants, best music scene and most ethnically diverse population, and it's the economic engine driving the region. Moreover, it is the most sustainable of the three cities based on our criteria.

But Dallas isn't content to be a big fish in the big state of Texas. The city is taking steps to be more competitive with all of the 50 major US cities we ranked, and has developed a comprehensive plan called Forward Dallas! outlining its strategies.

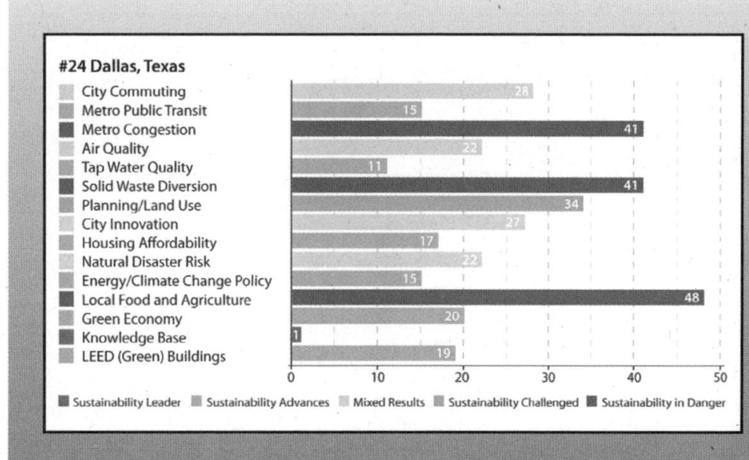

Healthy Living

Residents in Dallas enjoy reasonably good water (#11) and have a decent number of parks to play in (#18). The air is middling at #22. Despite (or maybe because of) being ringed and intersected by freeways much like the spokes of a wheel, Dallas suffers from serious traffic congestion (#41) that contributes to lower air quality during summer.

Although Dallas residents enjoy eating out an average of three nights per week, they haven't caught on to farmers' markets. Only one market is registered with the US Department of Agriculture. Slightly better is the opportunity for public urban gardening, with eight community gardens located within the city limits. Nonetheless, the city ranks #48 overall for local food and agriculture.

Getting Around

Making Dallas a less car-oriented city is a major thrust of the Forward Dallas! initiative. It won't be easy — just because the light rail system exists doesn't mean people will use it, and based on 2004 data, just over

4 percent commute to work on public transit. When commute ridership is below 5 percent, public transit is perceived as more of a novelty than a reliable form of transportation.

Bicycling and walking can be difficult. As a *Dallas Morning News* editorial put it, "Dallas is a city built for cars, not for people. If you doubt it, consider this: Virtually every street is lighted, but almost no sidewalks [are]. That's because people are expected to drive even short distances rather than walk." The DART (Dallas Rapid Transit) rail system is slated to double in size by 2014; it will be telling whether the system sees a significant increase in ridership.

The city is heading in the right direction with its vehicle fleet — biodiesel is regularly used as an alternative fuel.

Economic Factors

Dallas made the transition from an oil-based economy during the 1980s to become the "Silicon Prairie." Texas Instruments had already been a player in this industry since 1957, when the integrated circuit was invented. The retail industry also has a major presence; in fact, Dallas has more shopping centers per capita than any US city. Retail isn't famous for its contributions to sustainability, since its vast parking lots enable ongoing auto dependence and non-point water pollution from runoff.

The city's strategy for future economic development is to focus on what it can control — namely land use through zoning codes. New development is slated to increase density in most urban areas and preserve much of the 18 percent undeveloped land as open space. New city buildings will conform to LEED building standards, and landscaping will mitigate the heat island effect generated by the acres of concrete of the typical urban environment. Green roof replacement is another strategy in the mix.

Zoning alone may not be enough. Tax revenues will increase as energy-efficient buildings go up, but Dallas needs to do more to provide incentives for developing clean technology, such as renewable energy and production of biofuels. The city is heading in the right direction with its vehicle fleet — biodiesel is regularly used as an alternative fuel. Overall, the city fleet has 39 percent alternative-fueled vehicles, one of the highest rates in our study.

Summary/Next Steps

The city government has involved the community in creating a path toward greater sustainability. It already has a comprehensive Environmentally Preferable Purchasing plan, and is working on implementing an Environmental Management System in 11 city departments. The newly created Office of Environmental Quality will oversee the system.

Dallas will soon complete its greenhouse gas inventory, and it has a number of other interesting projects in the works, including using a bioreactor at the landfill to produce methane as fuel. Organizations such as Sustainable Dallas are working with the city to help kick-start sustainable ventures. Developing a local food infrastructure and aggressively promoting recycling — Dallas ranks #41 in waste diversion — are two things the city can do to move forward at an even faster pace.

25

Los Angeles, California

Significant Progress

Unhealthy inland air, poor tap water imported from afar, and semi-paralyzed roadways are enduring Los Angeles hallmarks, but the city has made significant progress toward becoming more sustainable.

For example, LA lords atop the recycling rankings (along with three other cities), and its five percent renewable energy use is surpassed by few US cities. A new commitment to bus rapid transit and light rail have kept commuter use close to 10 percent, helping LA earn a surprising #8 ranking in regional public transit. While the city is exploring ways in which such efforts will provide new jobs and greater freedom from imported fossil fuels, maintaining a high quality of life remains LA's most elusive challenge.

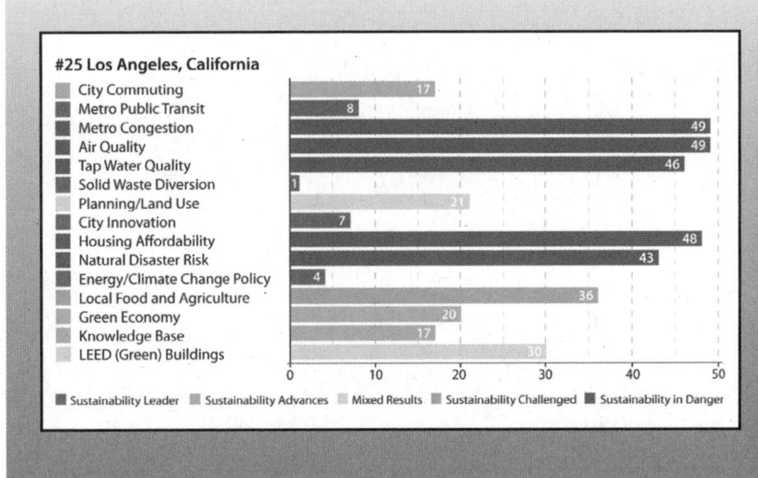

Healthy Living

Healthy alternatives are available not only on the coast, but all over town. Tap water and ocean sewage issues aside — the city's tap water comes in last out of the largest US cities, with 46 pollutants overall and 7 over the recommended threshold — Los Angeles has improved its air quality significantly since the infamous brown days of the 1960s and 1970s. Nevertheless, LA (both city and county) still ranks last overall in air quality, with "severe" ozone violations, "serious" carbon monoxide violations, and "serious" particulate matter violations, according to the EPA.

Hollywood's Griffith Park is a rambling, rocky mass of mountain, fern dens and spring creeks with honest-to-goodness coyotes lurking up around the famous sign and beyond. You can jog or ride a mountain bike there in solitude during weekdays and look out toward the ocean or east into Pasadena and the San Gabriel range. The coast is fine, too, with a nice paved trail running from Santa Monica to Venice Beach for running, biking or skating. Cycling in traffic is not for newbies, though, or even hardcore types—you'll see few cyclists on the streets, even around the campus of UCLA.

Nearby Santa Monica has the best farmers' markets, but LA does also offer quite a range, including some classic stands in the downtown area, with two year-round locations.

Getting Around

Eavesdrop on just about any conversation in Los Angeles and you'll learn that getting from point A to point B is never simple. Knowing what road to take and when is an essential skill in the city with the worst freeway and road congestion in the nation. Still, the city maintains a decent commute-to-work rate on public transit (near 10 percent), and LA is successfully criss-crossed with a Bus Rapid Transit system of

many miles and routes. Carpools are an option for many (about 10 percent use them) and the city offers both carpool coordination and car-sharing through private companies.

Economic Factors

Housing is some of the least affordable in the nation (#48), and the city's combined earthquake risk and precarious dependence on imported water may someday project it into any number of potential environmental disasters (LA ranks #43 in natural disaster risk).

Green building (#30) remains insignificant compared to what's happening in leading cities. Los Angeles does excel in renewable energy (#4), which makes up 5 percent of its energy mix. LA also has the most aggressive greenhouse-gas reduction target of any US city: 30 percent from 1999 to 2010. An impressive 25 percent of the vehicles in the city fleet run on alternative fuel.

Interstate 110 at dusk. This sprawling landscape has encouraged a car-dependent lifestyle.

PHOTO COURTESY LOS ANGELES CONVENTION AND VISITOR BUREAU

LA also has the most aggressive greenhouse-gas reduction target of any US city: 30 percent from 1999 to 2010.

Summary/Next Steps

The city's new commitment to renewable energy and recycling are two bright spots, as are attempts to increase public transit with light rail, subway and bus rapid transit. SustainLA is a project devoted to improving coordination among the city agencies that manage those systems.

LA's freeway and road congestion, though, is a painful everyday situation that wastes fuel, cuts productive hours for the workforce and even limits businesses' ability to get supplies in a timely manner. The eternally packed freeways are what playwright Sam Shepard likened to a giant ravenous serpent — and it shows no signs of being tamed.

The City of Angels must continue to improve public transit systems and increase ridership, facilitate more carpooling and car-sharing and develop more densely designed walkable areas similar to those in its "new downtown" to make the city economically competitive. The city currently facilitates carpooling only for city employees.

Water is another ongoing issue. TreePeople, a nonprofit, is working to help retain rainwater that the city and Army Corps of Engineers currently send through sewers to the open sea. Parks serve as 100,000-gallon flood-control catch basins with underground cisterns; the solution beautifies and also cools down neighborhoods. Unless innovative solutions like TreePeople's succeed, water is going to have to continue coming from far away, at great expenditures of energy and to the detriment of its quality.

26

Colorado Springs, Colorado

Growing Up Smart

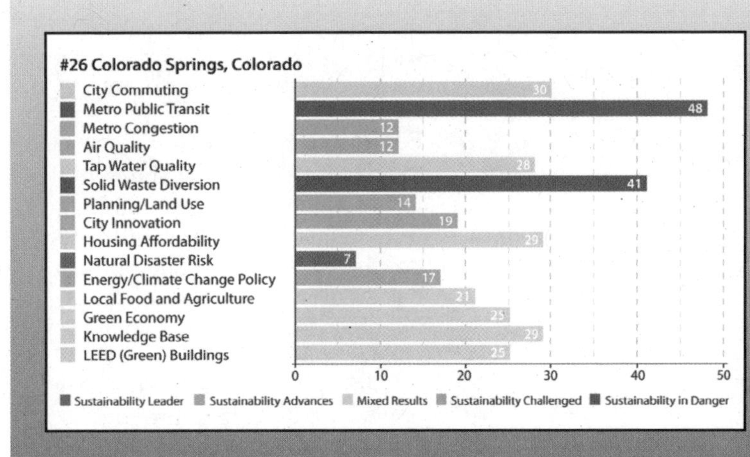

Nestled in the evening shadow of Pike's Peak, Colorado Springs has long been a place to kick back and enjoy the Rocky Mountain scenery. Set up in 1871 as a resort town, today Colorado Springs has over 360,000 people and a steady stream of visitors. Many of the area's early arrivals came to cash in on gold discovered at Cripple Creek and Victor in 1891. Many of those who hit pay dirt built monumental homes in the North End, still a posh section of town.

By 1917, the gold was gone. The next big economic boom came during World War II. Following the Pearl Harbor attack, Camp Carson was built, marking the beginning of a military boom-bust cycle — expansion during wartime, followed by decline. The military presence was cemented when the United States Air Force Academy was sited here during the 1950s, and in 1963 when the North American Aerospace Defense Command (NORAD) bunkered itself inside nearby Cheyenne Mountain.

Healthy Living

Rife with clean mountain air (ranking #12) and stunning parklands and open spaces, Colorado Springs residents have always made outdoor fitness a priority. The city is reasonably compact and walkable, and it recently enacted a policy called Complete Streets to encourage walking and bicycling.

Having a few more farmers' markets and community gardens in the vicinity might encourage even more people to venture out into their communities — the city ranks #21 for local food and agriculture. Tap water ranks #28 — you might consider putting a filter on your tap.

Getting Around

Most people in Colorado Springs drive alone to work (78 percent), and another 11 percent carpool. Public transportation use is virtually nonexistent, though a few people do walk to work (almost 3 percent). Residents have identified improving transportation as the city's most important issue. Getting drivers and passengers out of their cars and into their communities is one of the goals of the city's mixed-use development plan, which attempts to combine business and residential districts. It will take some time for such policies to have a major effect on people's habits, however.

The city has an excellent opportunity to take advantage of its compact size and Rocky Mountain location to create a healthy place for its present and future residents.

Economic Factors

The military is the backbone of the local economy; tourism and high-tech companies such as Intel round out the picture. Colorado Springs has an average number of green buildings (#25) but that could change soon if the Pikes Peak Sustainability Indicator Project recommendations are followed. Developed by the US Army's Fort Carson Mountain Post, the plan sets out some ambitious goals for the post and its host, El Paso County (which includes Colorado Springs), such as eliminating solid and hazardous waste and air emissions, converting all operations to renewable energy sources, including vehicles, and conforming all buildings to the LEED Platinum standard.

The city has made a commitment to increase its use of energy from renewable sources and is also working to reduce greenhouse gas emissions.

Summary/Next Steps

Colorado Springs has experienced tremendous population growth and development in the past 20 years. Now among the 50 largest US cities, it has only recently begun to experience typical urban problems such as congestion, rising crime and deteriorating neighborhoods. The city has an excellent opportunity to take advantage of its compact size and Rocky Mountain location to create a healthy place for its present and future residents.

27

Las Vegas, Nevada

Viva?

Having recently celebrated its centennial, Las Vegas today sports world-class restaurants, entertainers and the legendary Strip. It's one of the fastest-growing US cities — booming 12 percent from 2000 to 2004 alone.

Las Vegas is undergoing a fast-forward version of the classic urban development pattern of exurban sprawl that has led other Sun Belt cities into complete dependence on the automobile. As oil prices rise, such a city configuration presents a greater economic challenge for residents and employers. Another stumbling block — which may be a blessing in disguise — is that the city is beginning to run up against federally owned land at its outer limits.

With fast, sprawling growth comes a host of negative economic, environmental and public health consequences: congestion, increased air pollution and asthma, rising obesity rates, depletion of water resources, and, underlying it all, increased energy consumption. So it's promising that work has started on Project CityCenter, a multibillion-dollar mixed-use development on the Strip (which is officially unincorporated Las Vegas) with an emphasis on "non-gambling features," hopefully heralding a more urban form of city planning for the region.

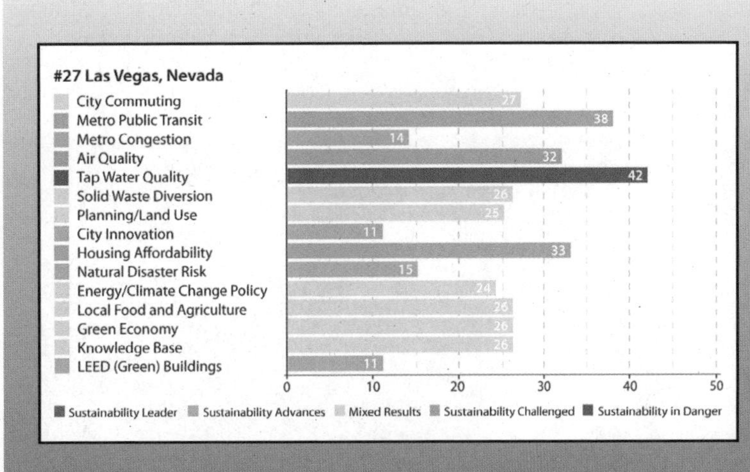

Healthy Living

Long known for its clear desert air, Las Vegas is now experiencing significant air pollution. The city's population boom and high rate of auto use have contributed to carbon monoxide pollution labeled "serious" by the EPA. The city ranks #32 in our study for air quality.

Tap water quality rates even further down the scale, coming in at #42 out of the largest 50 US cities. Water in Las Vegas contains 37 contaminants, 6 that are over the EPA recommended threshold. One ongoing threat is that the city needs to continually import water from more and more sources around the state, which may have varying degrees of water quality problems because of gold mining and other minimally regulated industrial activities.

Sin City doesn't exactly conjure images of fresh produce. But at least some of what's grown in Vegas stays in Vegas — the city has four farmers' markets. Las Vegas ranks just below average for local food indicators at #26.

Getting Around

In terms of commuting practices, Las Vegas falls behind most other US cities. About 4 percent use public transit to get to work, and less than 3 percent ride a bike or walk as part of their daily commute. About 76 percent drive alone to work, though the city does have an almost 13 percent carpool rate,

MGM Grand Casino, Las Vegas Strip.

PROPERTY OF MGM MIRAGE

which is in the top ten for that category.

In 2004 Las Vegas developed a monorail that connects the resorts along the Strip — though the Strip is not part of the City of Las Vegas proper. The city plans to invest in growing its bicycling infrastructure to get people out of their cars and onto human-powered transport.

Economic Factors

With about 300 sunny days a year, Las Vegas is a natural for solar power. Sponsored by two local utilities, the Green Power program enables ratepayers to make tax-deductible donations to finance solar projects. Residents may also participate in a net metering program, which allows property owners who have installed renewable energy systems on their property to sell power back to the grid.

Currently ranked at #11 in green (LEED) buildings per capita, Las Vegas is poised to become a leader in this high-growth sector of the economy. Although it has no LEED Certified buildings to date, 14 buildings are LEED Registered, including the Project CityCenter in Clark County. This vast entity will take up 66 acres — LEED certification and a denser configuration will help shrink its energy footprint. The fact that it's a multibillion-dollar complex in Vegas will also make other local and national developers take note.

Las Vegas leads the pack in its percentage of alternative-fueled city vehicles. In this era of impending oil shortages and rising gasoline prices, Las Vegas's fleet includes 450 biodiesel-powered vehicles, 268 compressed natural gas vehicles, a few hybrid cars, and even two Segway scooters being piloted for parking enforcement. The Clark County school district is also a leader in biodiesel use.

Las Vegas leads the pack in its percentage of alternative-fueled city vehicles.

Summary/Next Steps

Despite a reputation as an environmental dead zone, Las Vegas is making headway in engineering its future around more intelligent uses of resources. Besides green buildings, alternative-fueled vehicles, and utility net metering for residents to resell their solar power, Las Vegas has made an important move toward conserving the vast amounts of water it uses. The city opened a water reclamation facility in 2001 that can recycle 10 million gallons of water per day, which will help the desert city famed for its lavish waterfalls better conserve the wet stuff. If the city can start to use solar cells to power all those neon signs, light bulbs and casinos, Las Vegas might have a real sustainability story to tell.

28

Cleveland, Ohio

Give and Take on the Lake

Cleveland, which ranks #28, is no stranger to the consequences of unsustainable practices. The modern environmental movement literally blazed into public consciousness here during the late 1960s, when the polluted Cuyahoga River, which flows through the city into Lake Erie, caught fire. Repeatedly. Lake Erie, the fourth-largest Great Lake, was declared a "Dead Lake" in the 1970s, after pollution had caused algae to bloom in such quantity that fish populations died en masse. Now the river no longer lights up the night and Lake Erie, though still subject to a seasonal dead zone in its middle, supports sport fishing and healthy aquatic populations.

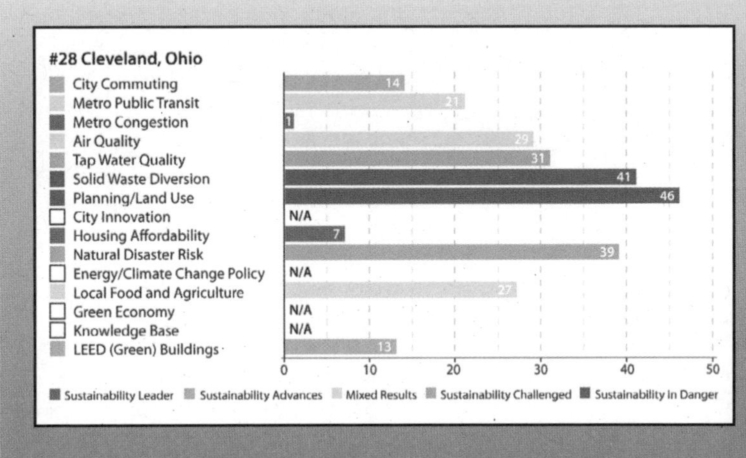

Besides its lakefront location, Cleveland has advantages over other large cities in Ohio in that it has good public transportation combined with a historic downtown that has been undergoing continual revitalization since the 1980s. The bad news is that the city continues to lose population to its suburbs and other parts of the nation: The city's population declined from 914,000 in 1950 to 458,000 in 2004.

Healthy Living

Cleveland gets middle-of-the-road marks in most healthy living categories, including #29 in air quality and #31 in tap water quality. Lake Erie supplies plentiful water, but not all of it is savory. The city's tap water contains 19 contaminants, including 4 over the recommended EPA threshold.

For parks, the city also rates below average — its 5.8 percent parkland (out of total city acreage) puts it at #35 in that category. You can, however, spend years exploring Lakefront State Park, created in the 1970s when four city parks were combined into a single "super park" connected by a bicycle path and fitness course.

Cleveland's metro area public transit ranks above average in both its city commuter rates (#14) and in its regional transit ridership (#21).

Overall, the city ranks #27 in local food and agriculture, with a high rate of community gardens — there are about 200 — offset by only two farmers' markets.

Getting Around

Cleveland's metro area public transit ranks above average in both its city commuter rates (#14) and in its regional transit ridership (#21). About 8.3 percent of Clevelanders ride public transit, and just over 4 percent walk to work. Biking to work is almost nonexistent, at 0.1 percent. The carpooling rate, at 11.7 percent, is higher than average. Still, more than 72 percent of residents drive alone to work, a higher rate than, for example, Los Angeles's 70 percent. Despite this, Cleveland's metro area remains the least traffic-congested city in our study.

Economic Factors

Industry in Cleveland still conforms to a typical Rustbelt profile: chemical and food processing; some steel, electrical products and auto parts manufacturing; and printing and publishing. Other economic opportunities include the city's newer status as a regional and national tourist attraction. In addition to the lakefront, the city is known for the Cleveland Metropolitan Orchestra, the Rock and Roll Hall of Fame and some famous pro sports teams.

Green building appears to be making fast progress, with the city's ten LEED Registered buildings ranking it #13. The city is the eighth most affordable of the 50 largest US cities.

Summary/Next Steps

Cleveland started a Sustainability Program within its water department in 2005. The program, which was staffed with one person at the time of our survey, is responsible for developing alternative fuels in the city fleet and investigating the use of renewable energy. The successful growth in green building appears to be a partial result of the program's incentives and guidance.

If it wants to move faster toward sustainability, there are a number of actions Cleveland can take. To complement its ongoing urban historic district redevelopment, Cleveland might consider encouraging the development of more parks, farmers' markets and clean technology businesses.

29

Miami, Florida

Gateway of the Americas

Miami seems to face away from North America in more ways than one. Nearly 75 percent of its residents speak something other than English at home. There are numerous expat and immigrant enclaves — Hispanic, Caribbean, French, Finnish, South African, Turkish, Russian, Jewish and others. Add to this some affluent northeasterners in search of sunbelt, and you get a peculiar, vibrant mélange of cultures.

Multinational businesses headquarter their Latin American operations in Miami, where plenty of international financial transactions take place. But economics goes one way, nature another.

Behind its bejeweled seaside façade, a sprawling city maintains a precarious foothold on the edge of the Everglades swamp. This vast sheet of slow-draining wetland is the subject of an anxious public works effort — one of the most extensive in the nation — to urge water along networks of canals and levees so that the swamp doesn't swell into floodplain. Indeed, Miami, sandwiched between two intensely active hurricane regions, is more vulnerable to natural disaster than any other city in our study. Michael Grunwald chronicles how precarious the city's history and current existence is in *The Swamp: the Everglades, Florida and the Politics of Paradise.*

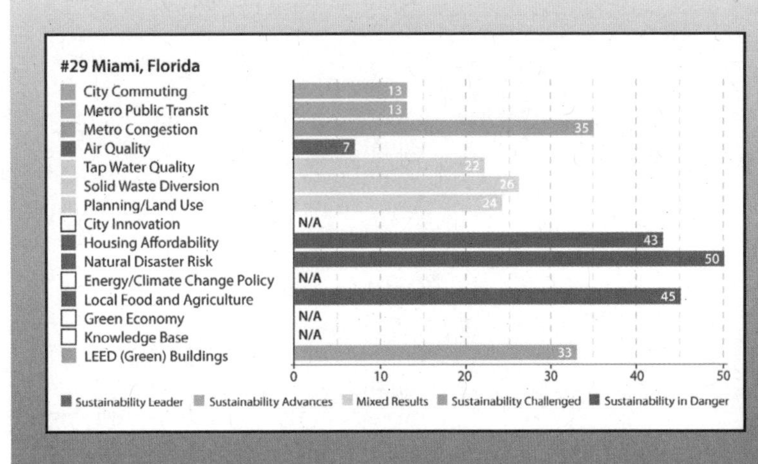

Healthy Living

The city's traditional selling points — sunshine, leisure, beach parties — are helping to fuel a phenomenal real estate boom. Luxury towers with brand names like Trump are multiplying in Miami — so many that maxed-out contractors are turning clients away. By some estimates, 40,000 new condo units are on their way. And buyers are lining up.

Who could blame them? With its oceanfront locale and open skies, Miami can boast a superior quality of life. Its air quality ranks #7 in our study. Its tap water is decent overall (#22). But testing this water reveals an unhealthy level of selenium. Selenium is persistent in areas denuded by sprawl or too much industry, and new urban developments may further tax Miami's aquifer. South Florida residents already use more water per person than any other city in the nation.

With its oceanfront locale and open skies, Miami can boast a superior quality of life.

Meanwhile, there seems to be low priority given to improving sustainable basics like local food — Miami ranks #45 in the food and agriculture category. Miami is also behind the curve in parkland (#40).

Getting Around

Miami has a good public transportation system, with city ridership ranking #13 in our study. Rail and bus serve the city and its outlying metro area, and downtown boasts an automated people-mover (much like the short rail circuits at airports), with arrivals every 90 seconds during peak usage. About 11 percent of Miami residents carpool, an average figure in our study, while city road and highway congestion ranks #35, due in part to the nation's least-dense office distribution. Business space is not concentrated in downtown proper or even at the edge of the city; people drive farther in all directions to get to work, which means a trend toward more roadways and highways.

Economic Factors

Miami comes in at #33 for green building. For all the new construction, very little of it seems to strive for LEED standards. LEED guidance informs not just how efficiently a building works during its lifespan, but also how its initial construction proceeds. So far, there are no indications that the thousands of condo and office units being added each year are green.

There are some efforts to seed green building here, though. For instance, a nonprofit called Florida Green Housing funds low-income residential construction that adheres to standards of sustainability. And in early 2006, Miami hosted a conference on sustainable building, Tropical Green, that received major accolades. If these efforts don't influence the current construction boom, which some fear is a bubble, there may not be capital left over to go green when the dust settles and air-conditioning energy costs skyrocket.

Summary/Next Steps

Miami receives high marks for superior air quality and decent transit options, but has an unfocused approach to sustainability. Known as the Gateway of the Americas, it has an opportunity to set the example for Latin and South American development. Currently, the city is developing a luxury skyline, despite the fact it fronts the coast of the most dangerous hurricane zone in the nation. If Miami wishes to make a statement about the future of the Americas, it might consider developing a comprehensive sustainability plan now to better shape the current transformation of its urban space.

30

Long Beach, California

A Sea of Opportunities

Of course, Long Beach is more than a port: It's a major city in its own right, with a population (500,000) larger than that of Atlanta or Cleveland. But the port's shadow on the city is significant, adversely affecting both air and water quality. The city of Long Beach and the state of California have been working intensely with the port to make its operations cleaner and more sustainable. With so many people living so close to such a major source of air pollution — ships typically burn a relatively unclean type of diesel fuel — Long Beach's green port initiatives are an important step toward making the city as livable as its more upscale coastal neighbors.

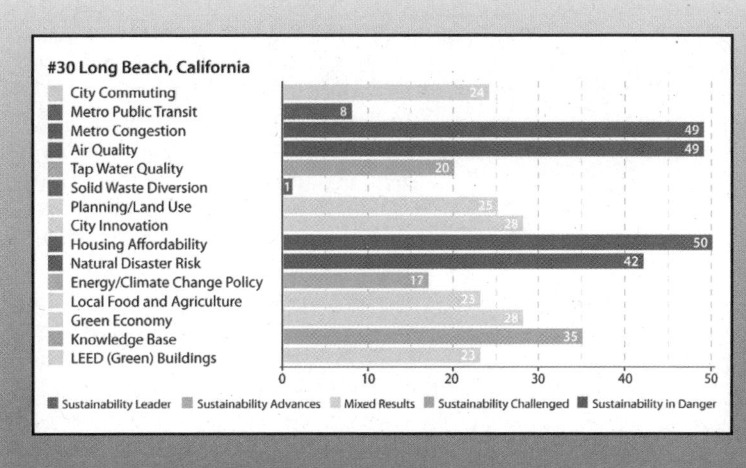

Healthy Living

Long Beach is tied for last in air quality. Like Los Angeles, Long Beach gets air pollution from the Santa Ana winds blowing from inland, but because of the ship traffic, it also gets polluted air from the sea. One ship can produce as much pollution as 12,000 cars. The city and port are working with shipping companies, most of them based outside the United States, to use less-polluting fuels and electric generators, as Seattle's port is doing with some shipping lines.

In 2006, the Port of Long Beach began a six-year, $2.5 million tree-planting effort, which will help provide more oxygen, reduce temperatures, and help prevent polluted water from running off into the ocean.

The tap water quality in this city rates much higher than that of nearby Los Angeles, coming in at #20. The city gets a fair amount from local underground aquifers and the ocean, with one of the nation's largest desalinization plants. Tap water includes 13 contaminants, 2 of which are over the recommended threshold.

Long Beach ranks #21 in percent of park acreage, and the city has four farmers' markets for fresh local produce.

Getting Around

Part of the L.A. Basin, Long Beach is entangled in the most congested roadway and freeway system in the country. All those semi trucks leaving the port don't help matters. Over 76 percent of Long Beach residents drive alone to work, compared to LA's 70.6 percent.

The city is hard-pressed to come up with a solution to increase public transit ridership above its current 7.5 percent rate. Redeveloping more walkable neighborhoods and business districts would help relieve traffic problems, as would any city-sponsored carpooling or carsharing programs.

Economic Factors

Long Beach has some elements of a green economy in place, including 4 percent renewable energy and a slightly above-average ranking (#23) for green buildings. A sizeable green city fleet (with 18 percent using alternative fuels) presents possibilities for boosting local clean tech industries through pilot programs.

What the city lacks, however, is a focused effort to collaborate with federal research agencies or non-governmental organizations on the development of innovative, sustainable economic development programs or projects.

Summary/Next Steps

Long Beach's efforts to limit the environmental impacts of its port are important. A next step might be to create an overall plan for sustainability. Creating green building incentives and a greenhouse gas reduction plan, for example, would put the city on par with most other leading West Coast port cities, and Seattle, Portland and San Francisco could all offer good models. The city's port location makes it a natural for clean tech manufacturing incubation that could create local jobs and reduce the air pollutants Long Beach residents now breathe.

JON SULLIVAN / PDPHOTO.ORG

Port of Long Beach with downtown skyline. The city faces urgent challenges from the port's numerous sources of air pollution.

31

El Paso, Texas

Bordering on Sustainability

El Paso's first century was based on booming mining and minerals processing, but for the past 30 years, downtown El Paso has been marked by a downhill slide in economics and quality of life. Now the city is undertaking a Downtown Plan to revitalize its city center.

You'll find much to like in El Paso. In addition to its unique bi-national culture, the city is affordable, features many parks and has a moderate climate for much of the year, at almost 4,000 feet in the high desert near the Franklin Mountains. A renewed Plaza Theater and several downtown museums, part of the Bi-National Arts Walk, are soon to be joined, by a mixed-use business and residential neighborhood. Open-air plazas, a key cultural attraction in Latin America and the Southwest, are also poised for a comeback.

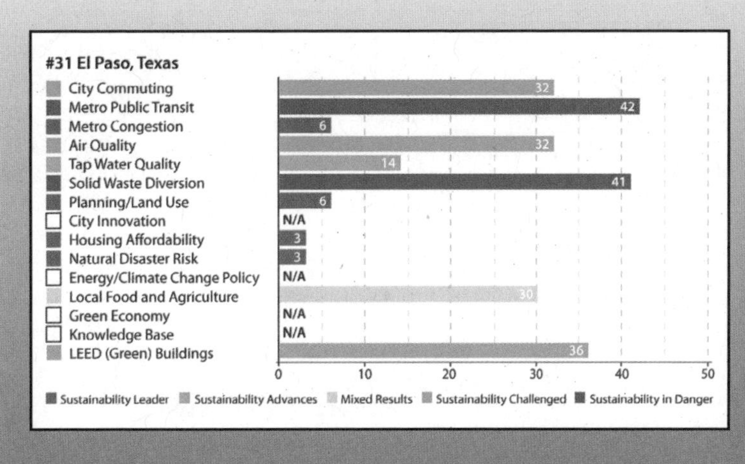

Healthy Living

El Paso's air quality ranks #32 out of the largest 50 US cities. Tap water comes from local aquifers and the Rio Grande. Drinking water quality is ranked #14 — it contains 20 contaminants, including 2 that exceed the EPA's recommended threshold. The city ranks #30 for local food and agriculture, with 5 farmers' markets and 12 community gardens.

The city's 175 parks are an area of particular civic strength — El Paso uses 16.5 percent of its land for parks, placing it at #6. The Franklin Mountains State Park is one of the largest urban parks in the nation, at 24,000 acres. You can enjoy rock climbing and 118 miles of trails for horseback riding, hiking and mountain biking.

Getting Around

The city ranks #32 in commuting, with less than 3 percent riding public transit to work and under 4 percent walking or biking to work. About 77 percent of El Paso's residents drive by themselves to work, which is above the national average. Less than 4 percent bike or walk to work.

El Paso is making the transition from dirtier mining and metals processing industries to cleaner industries.

Economic Factors

El Paso is affordable (#3) and has little need to fear major natural disasters (#3), despite the downtown flooding that occurred in mid-2006. The city is making the transition from dirtier mining and metals processing industries to cleaner industries. The largest employers are the military, the US government (the Department of Customs and the Drug Enforcement Agency), schools, call centers and textile manufacturers.

For green (LEED) building, El Paso ranks #36, with 3 LEED Registered buildings as of the first quarter of 2006.

Summary/Next Steps

A much more extensive public transit system would help El Paso take advantage of its urban redesign and historic preservation efforts. The city's historic district has great potential as a neighborhood with a distinct cultural identity, which should be appealing to shoppers, residents and tourists.

Because of El Paso's sunny high-desert elevation, solar and wind energy could be good industries to attract for both local energy production and for regional export.

The city's proximity to Ciudad Juarez helps the metro area form the largest community on the US-Mexico border, with 2.5 million in combined population. Officials from both cities have an opportunity to collaboratively address shared environmental issues relating to air and water quality, in addition to regional transportation. A model for such planning includes cross-border collaboration in San Diego and its southern neighbor, Tijuana, with the *San Diego Dialogue* and *El Colegio de la Frontera Norte.*

32

New Orleans, Louisiana

Resiliently Facing the Future

Katrina demonstrates the role natural disaster risk plays in a city's sustainability: Nobody knows quite what the city's future holds. Will the estimated half of the city's population displaced by the hurricane return? Can it shore up its levee system enough in advance of future storms? Will businesses relocate in the beleaguered city?

What is known is that the city is resiliently looking to its future. New Orleans city officials, who have collaborated with SustainLane to provide data for this study in the wake of Katrina, recognize the importance of sustainability and environmental management. These will be important considerations as the city builds for its future: New Orleans is situated below sea level on a Mississippi River Delta floodplain. While the following statistics draw on pre-Katrina New Orleans (except where noted), we intend them to serve as helpful reference points that support the city's rebuilding.

The principles of sustainability are not new to New Orleans. By 2001, New Orleans business, civic and social leaders had already started developing a long-term process called Top Ten by 2010 that aspired to increase social equity, promote economic development, and clean up the environment. These remain issues the city has an opportunity to address.

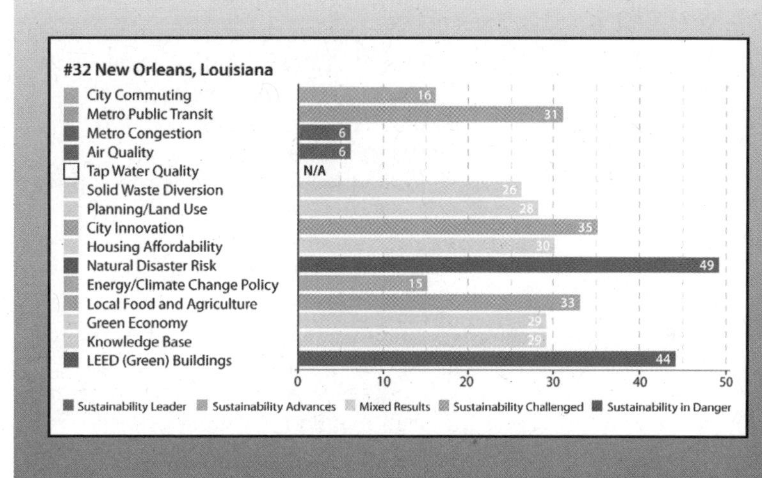

Healthy Living

While it may be hot and humid, the air quality in New Orleans is very good, ranking #6, though residents should be mindful of the mold, contaminants in the soil, and food contamination caused by 2005's Katrina flooding. Tap water quality was not included in the city water quality database SustainLane used for ranking purposes (the Environmental Working Group's

From the cane-chaired vintage streetcars of the Garden District to the inexpensive ferries of Algiers, New Orleans features charming and well-maintained public transit options.

2005 database), but the Natural Resource Defense Council did rate New Orleans tap water quality as "good" in a 2001 national study. In May 2006, the state Health Department said water was safe to drink in the Ninth Ward, which received the heaviest flood damage.

New Orleans ranks #33 for local food and agriculture, with 4 farmers' markets and 54 community gardens pre-Katrina. As of May 2006, two of the four farmers' markets were open, and 22 community gardens had been restored and planted, according to Parkway Partners, the largest privately funded neighborhood gardens project in the nation.

Getting Around

From the cane-chaired vintage streetcars of the Garden District to the inexpensive ferries of Algiers, New Orleans features charming and well-maintained public transit options. It ranks #16 for commuting overall, with just under 12 percent commuting by public transit. Road and freeway congestion (#6) is not much of an issue for drivers in the metro region.

Economic Factors

New Orleans and re-elected Mayor Ray Nagin face tough questions about how to redevelop its economic base following Hurricane Katrina. There are competing visions for the city's future, and significant conflicts, such as whether the lowest-lying neighborhoods, including the Ninth Ward, should be redeveloped at all.

Three key questions are likely to determine the shape of New Orleans's future economy: Will tourists return in large numbers? Will small businesses return? Will another hurricane hit? The first two questions are impossible to answer until the city rebuilds. In regard to the third question, the city ranks #49 for natural disaster risk (only Miami has a greater risk rating), so substantial efforts must go into building new levees and pumping facilities for it to avoid a repeat of Katrina.

Summary/Next Steps

New Orleans is a challenged city that must turn to sustainable approaches to ensure its survival. Doing so may well involve drawing upon lessons from the Dutch — who have successfully lived below sea level for hundreds of years — and upon the best knowledge in environmental land and water management practices.

The city's first priority is to create a secure situation for itself. This will involve plenty of pumps and levee engineering. New Orleans and the state of Louisiana also have an opportunity to build up the delta with reclaimed barrier islands, marshes, ridges and wetlands, which would provide protection against future hurricanes. The Pontchartrain Coastal Lines of Defense Program is designed to do just that. This comprehensive plan offers an ecological and economic solution for the decades-long loss of coastal buffer zone due to coastal development and the Army Corps of Engineers' artificial channeling of the Mississippi, which has sent sediment out to sea instead of across the river's flood plain.

33

Fresno, California

Nature's Bounty

Beyond the major beef and dairy produced, fruit and vegetables of almost every sort are grown in the San Joaquin Valley, which produces more than 250 types of commercial crops. If you're eating produce right now, there's a good chance it came through Fresno.

Immigrants and migrant workers from countries all over the globe convene in Fresno, giving it a great diversity of people, food and cultural activities. Cultures vary from Hmong (11 percent of the population) to Latino (40 percent) to communities of Armenian and Ukrainian descent.

If you're a nature enthusiast, you'll appreciate Fresno's proximity to some of the nation's most famous national parks. It's a perfect base for visiting Yosemite, Sequoia, and Kings Canyon.

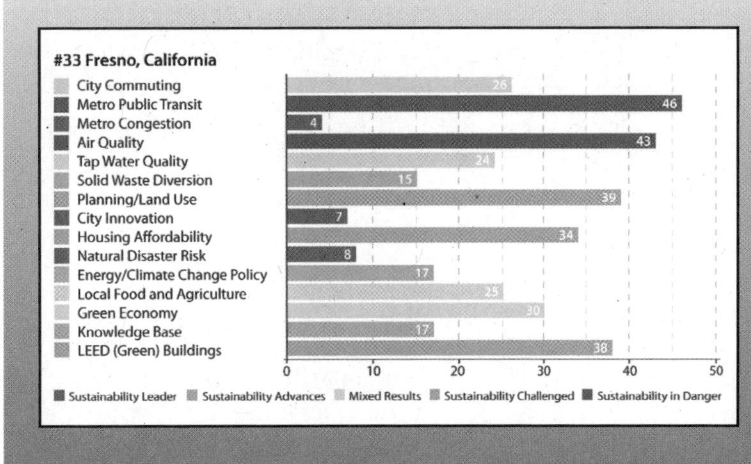

Healthy Living

In an area with so much food grown locally, you might expect a potpourri of farmers' markets scattered across the city. There are, in fact, only 3 farmers' markets and 15 community gardens. There is a unique gardening center, the Mokichi Okada Center, that farms according to strict standards of purity. In addition to Japanese tea ceremonies and flower arranging, the center has orchards and sells fruits and vegetables, including baskets of pesticide-free local strawberries.

The water quality in Fresno is questionable, with 31 contaminants, 3 of which are over the recommended limit (#24). Because Fresno sits at the bottom of a valley backed up against the Sierra in the west and the Tehachapi Mountains to the south, polluted air from Los Angeles and the whole Central Valley — which can be heavily contaminated with pesticides from industrial agriculture and ground-level ozone dairy methane emissions — get pushed over to Fresno (#43 in air quality). The city has numerous air quality warning days during the summer, when temperatures can reach the 100s.

With air pollution worsening in the San Joaquin Valley, in 2005 the valley's Air District passed a $780 development fee on all new homes being built. Developers can reduce the fee by adding sidewalks, bike lanes, landscaping and energy-efficient appliances. Such a step could help protect the city from the valley's worrisome air pollution, which some predict will soon surpass that of even the Los Angeles Basin.

Once neglected, downtown Fresno has seen significant growth and private investment since the 1990s.

Getting Around

Once neglected, downtown Fresno has seen significant growth and private investment since the 1990s. Several of the old neighborhoods are now restored, vital communities. The Tower District, for example, has been transformed into a vibrant, culturally diverse area of shops, homes, restaurants, nightclubs and bookstores. At the same time, the city continues to grow outward, encouraging auto travel and providing little public transportation.

Only 3 percent of the population use public transit to commute to work, and another 3 percent walk or ride a bike. With 77 percent driving alone and 12 percent carpooling, the city ranks #26 in commuting and #46 in metro public transit ridership. On a brighter note, the city vehicle fleet has more than 13 percent alternative-fueled vehicles.

Economic Factors

Agriculture is the backbone of the Fresno economy, providing more than $3.5 billion dollars annually. Major crops include grapes, cotton, cattle, tomatoes, milk, plums, oranges, tangerines and peaches. More jobs are tied to agriculture than to any other industry in Fresno, which has recently seen the emergence of a large processing industry.

With a diverse bounty of locally grown food that employs such a large percentage of the population, Fresno has a head start toward becoming a truly sustainable community. Unfortunately, most of the agricultural jobs are not very stable or high-paying, and most of the food leaves the area to be distributed around the world.

The city offers some incentives for green building, but LEED buildings are scarce (#38). Renewable energy used in the city's energy mix includes solar and geothermal.

Summary/Next Steps

Fresno is faced with a conundrum. It's sited near natural wonders, but citizens have few of their own parks. Tremendous amounts of locally produced agriculture abound, yet there are only three farmers' markets. Agriculture brings in billions to the local economy, yet the air and water can be polluted with pesticides and diesel emissions from tractors and trucks. The downtown is strengthening, but there is continued sprawl.

Fortunately, with nature's bounty so near, Fresno has a great opportunity to quickly become more sustainable. Fresno can readily tap its locally grown food supply, including small farms producing organics, which don't pollute air and water with pesticides. Developing more parks and public transit would be another way to keep people in town and reduce pollution.

34

Charlotte, North Carolina

New Alternatives in the Pipeline

Charlotte is one of the fastest-growing cities in the United States. This growth includes large subdivisions emerging on the edges of town. At the same time, the state, county and city government, along with many residents, have recognized the importance of limiting sprawl by using "smart growth." The ideas behind smart growth are to increase public transportation, improve air quality, and encourage infill in the core of the city.

As in so many other US cities, downtown Charlotte declined as the suburbs grew. That's changing as public and private funding starts to reach older neighborhoods. From warehouse districts like South End, which was converted into residential lofts, restaurants and shops, to historic preservation projects like Myers Park (the first suburb served by streetcars), the center of the city is being transformed. It's now home to a vibrant mix of young professionals, artists, empty nesters and the well-to-do. This trend coincides with an effort to increase public transportation across the metro region in Mecklenburg County.

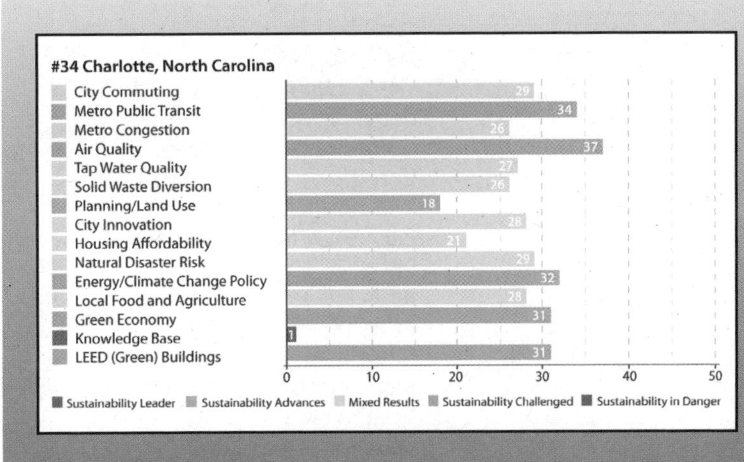

Healthy Living

In both air and water quality, Charlotte receives low scores. The tap water (#27) has 15 contaminants, 4 of which exceed the recommended limit, and the air quality (#37) is poor. Both of these concerns are at the forefront of smart growth impacts. The Environmental Leadership Policy for Mecklenburg County highlights air quality as the most urgent environmental concern. They also recognize that air quality is part of a larger growth management issue.

Many city officials are starting to realize that negative ecological feedback loops might actually hurt development. An April 2006 article in *The Charlotte Observer* noted that "more development means more pavement, which increases dirty runoff, which hurts water quality, which ultimately hinders development."

Local produce is not one of the primary areas targeted in any of the smart growth plans. The city has 4 farmers' markets. Its 17 community gardens demonstrate some awareness of the economic and health benefits of local food production.

In 1998, a voter-approved half-cent sales tax enabled the city to improve and expand bus service. Since then, bus ridership has increased by 50 percent.

Getting Around

Continued sprawl has led to a heavy dependence on auto travel in Charlotte; 76 percent of the population drives to work alone. Mayor Pat McCrory has been trying to influence such habits for more than ten years. In 1998, a voter-approved half-cent sales tax enabled the city to improve and expand bus service. Since then, bus ridership has increased by 50 percent, with many of the new riders coming from the suburbs or exurbs.

Mayor McCrory has also championed light rail, which is scheduled to begin service in 2007. Development has already begun on the light rail hubs, with wide sidewalks to encourage foot traffic. Eight of the stations will be pedestrian-friendly; seven will have a large public park-and-ride bus. As of 2004, only 3.5 percent of the population commuted to work on public transit. New alternatives in the pipeline and support from public officials are likely to boost that number.

Economic Factors

Although it doesn't look like Charlotte has a very strong sustainable economy, several exciting trends are emerging. City officials are ready to help developers with projects in the city core, especially in infill areas and along transit corridors, with only one catch: They must score high enough on the city's sustainability index, which promotes smart growth. Although the criteria are vague and are not officially green building incentives, the requirement is evidence that the city is beginning to design sustainable development approaches.

At present, the city does not have renewable energy sources in its energy mix. One organization promoting renewable energy in North Carolina, NC Green Power, is an independent nonprofit organization established to improve North Carolina's environment through voluntary contributions to renewable energy including wind, water, solar and organic matter. In one of its programs, NC Green Power promotes green-powered events such as church functions, conferences, parties, weddings, concerts and festivals.

Summary/Next Steps

Charlotte has only just begun to address sprawl and its byproducts. Many of the city's smart growth projects are either in planning phases or mere infancy, and are focusing on getting the many communities throughout the metro region to agree on shared priorities. The Environmental Leadership Policy team has been assembled to address energy conservation, recycling, low-emission vehicles, land preservation and environmentally sensitive design.

The projects and initiatives beginning to emerge in public transit and development are signs that Charlotte is poised to make itself a more sustainable city. By broadening such efforts to include renewable energy and local food supply, Charlotte can make strides toward that goal.

Downtown Charlotte: jogging toward a less car-dependent future?

COURTESY KELLY OWEN / KJOPHOTO.COM

35

Louisville, Kentucky

City of Parks

Mayor Jerry Abramson, who enjoys tremendous support from the community (informally, he's known as "Mayor for Life"), has championed projects that support parks, local food and healthy living. He's worked hard to create strong neighborhoods and support local businesses. Over his tenure — he's the longest-standing mayor in Louisville's history — he's overseen the revitalization of downtown with waterfront parks, historic preservation districts and small local businesses and restaurants.

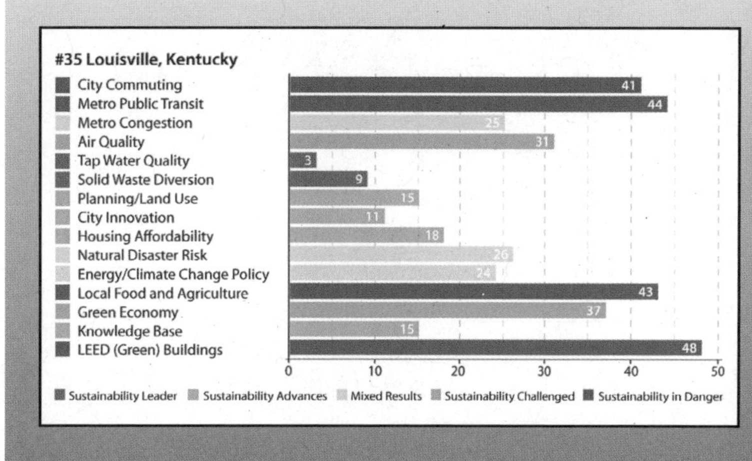

Healthy Living

Locals are fortunate to have excellent water quality (ranked #3), coming primarily from a local source, the Ohio River.

The Mayor's Healthy Hometown Movement is a novel program that aspires to increase the number of people in the city who exercise regularly and eat a healthy diet. Among other things, the program promotes farmers' markets. The city has two farmers' markets that meet the definition set by the USDA, which requires that goods are produced or grown locally and sold by the primary producer or somebody who works with the primary producer. In addition to the two official farmers' markets, there are more than 30 other local food markets.

Louisville ranks #35 in parkland, with 122 parks covering 14,000 acres, including three large parks and several smaller parks designed by 19th-century park visionary Frederick Law Olmsted. A new initiative called City of Parks should improve Louisville's ranking by creating thousands of acres of parks and paths in areas where land is rapidly being developed into subdivisions and shopping centers. The project will also connect the waterfront with many other parks in the city, including those designed by

Olmsted. Ultimately, walkways with biking and hiking trails will create a loop around the entire county (the City of Louisville and County of Jefferson became one entity through a merger in 1994).

Getting Around

At #44 in commute to work and #41 in regional public transportation, it's clear that Louisville residents are attached to auto travel. In fact, 82 percent of the population commutes to work alone in a car; 4 percent use public transit. A motorized trolley, the Toonerville II Trolley, ambles through downtown.

A forward-thinking mayor and proactive local community are pushing Louisville toward a more sustainable future.

Economic Factors

The Partnership for a Green Community, a formal collaborative effort between Louisville Metro, the University of Louisville and Jefferson County public schools focuses on environmental management, environmental education and environmental health issues. The goal is to create a greener, more sustainable community. The three partners employ 26,000 people, enroll 120,000 students, and own more than 500 buildings, 7,000 vehicles, and 25,000 acres of land. The partnership focuses on policy to address renewable energy, conservation, recycling, air pollution and other related issues. However, while this program encourages renewable energy, the city does not currently draw energy from renewable sources.

An extensive recycling and composting program has helped Louisville divert 46 percent of its waste (ranking #9), one of the higher rates in the Eastern US.

There are no commercial or residential green building incentives. However, according to an article in *Business First*, a local business journal, architects and clients in Louisville are embracing green principles such as energy efficiency, effective site orientation and recycled materials, with an overall goal to reduce natural resource consumption.

Summary/Next Steps

A forward-thinking mayor and proactive local community are pushing Louisville toward a more sustainable future. A commitment toward sustainability can be seen in the enthusiasm for a local food supply, plans for more parks, a high rate of waste diversion and a collaborative citywide project to educate and design projects incorporating healthier approaches for people and the economy.

The primary way that Louisville can strengthen its commitment to sustainability is by developing public transportation options, making it easier for people to get around without driving their cars. It also has to contend with sprawl, and has an opportunity to create a healthier environment by investing in renewable energy sources and creating incentives for green building and green businesses.

36

Jacksonville, Florida

Thinking Ahead

Road, river and rail meet the Atlantic at Jacksonville, Florida, which is host to a deepwater port and myriad transportation services. Jacksonville harbors freighters destined for Europe, South America and the Caribbean. It's also a national gateway for automobile shipping. Without much fanfare, Jacksonville is preparing for its financial future by gathering skilled professionals and Fortune 500 companies under its sign, including major insurance and banking concerns.

The city's business acumen hasn't come at the expense of its misty Southern charm. The ancient St. Johns River slides through the city's bulk, and a peculiar mossy drip infests the giant oaks. Framing these gothic scenes is a bustling modern infrastructure.

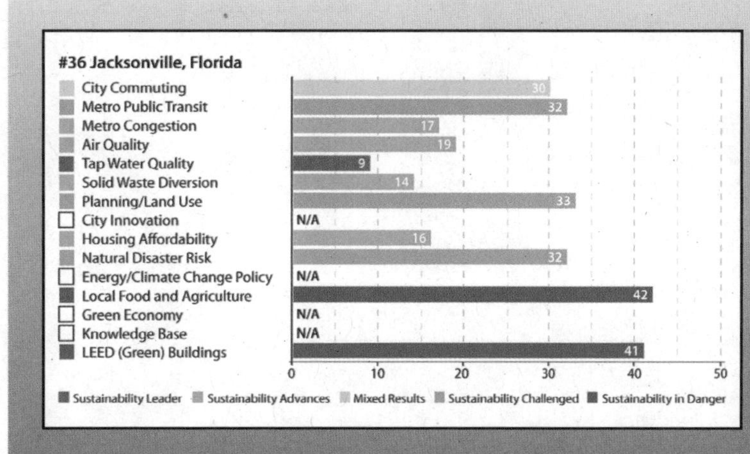

Healthy Living

Jacksonville has plenty of potential for healthy living: It has clean water (#9) from a deep underground aquifer and relatively healthy air (#19), with no violations of EPA Clean Air Act standards. Jacksonville also ranks better than average in park acreage (#20) — over 9 percent of the city's sprawling land is set aside for recreation.

But the city lacks a reliable source of local food and agriculture, which is curious, considering the region's year-round growing climate and plentiful, clean water supply. The city has only two farmers' markets and 19 community gardens, putting it at #42 for local food and agriculture.

Getting Around

In terms of its physical dimensions, Jacksonville has the largest city size in the nation. Nearly 800,000 people make their homes in the sprawling city, scattered over 800 square miles. Over 80 percent drive alone to work. What's more, recent trends indicate that more people are

COURTESY OF JACKSONVILLE & THE BEACHES CONVENTION AND VISITORS BUREAU

Automated Skyway Express, Jacksonville's downtown peoplemover.

commuting between rather than within counties in Northeastern Florida — the average commute is getting longer.

The city offers some alternatives to driving. An elevated rail system with 2.5 miles of track serves the downtown core, shuttling riders back and forth across the river within a small circuit. Bus routes handle the rest. Less than 2 percent of commuters use public transportation, one of the lower scores out of the 50 largest US cities.

To improve this situation, the Jacksonville Transportation Authority is reviewing a wider menu for city transit, including ferries on the St. Johns — the same waterway that over the decades has prompted the construction of five bridges for motor traffic. Another possibility involves new diesel-powered commuter trains that would run on existing freight rails. Meanwhile, a major transportation station is being planned that will connect the current elevated rail system to city buses, intercity Amtrak lines, and Greyhound buses. Perhaps with these improvements, Jacksonville can provide for residents and tourists the same flexible mobility it currently affords international cargo.

Economic Factors

Jacksonville is among the more affordable cities (#16) in our study. It also benefits from top-notch organizations that aim to make housing more affordable for disadvantaged groups. Neighborhood Housing Services of Jacksonville, for instance, facilitates loans and grants to revitalize Springfield, a large neighborhood north of downtown. Many of these loans help low-income households buy and remodel historic wood-frame houses, thus ensuring that neighborhood rescue doesn't automatically mean displacement through gentrification.

In a similar vein, Habitat for Humanity has been very active in Jacksonville, constructing houses for low-income families; the Jacksonville program is Habitat's largest in the country, and it has garnered specific praise from the US Department of Housing and Urban Development. Like most southeastern cities (Atlanta is the exception), Jacksonville shows little evidence of green building (#41).

The city is vulnerable to both hurricanes and flooding, ranking #32 for natural disaster risk.

Summary/Next Steps

Each year, the Jacksonville Community Council (JCCI) addresses specific problems confronting the city through study groups. Any citizen can volunteer to participate in the groups, whose findings are published by the council and publicized by advocacy programs. Since the early 1990s, the JCCI has been producing an annual Quality of Life Progress Report to assay the overall health of the city in terms of economics, education, environment, social equality, mobility and the arts.

The JCCI programs serve as a national model of citizen-powered, forward-thinking examination of local problems. (The explicit inclusion of energy conservation and other indicators of sustainability would make the efforts even more promising.) While Jacksonville may currently lag behind in our study, it already has a brain trust in place. If it can channel the indicators of the JCCI into city programs, policies and practices, Jacksonville might quickly climb the ranks of the nation's green cities.

Jacksonville is among the more affordable cities (#16) in our study. It also benefits from top-notch organizations that aim to make housing more affordable for disadvantaged groups.

37

Omaha, Nebraska

Encouraging Signs in the Heartland

Omaha lies almost smack dab in the center of the country, surrounded by cropland seeded on former prairie. The birthplace of TV dinners, Gerald Ford and Malcolm X features a local industry based on banking and insurance, food processing, construction, and telecommunications.

On the weekends, locals gather in Old Market, the arts and entertainment district, and on hot summer evenings you'll find folks strolling along the 31-acre Heartland of America Park, which fronts the Missouri River. The city is typically Midwestern: sedate, welcoming and predominantly suburban.

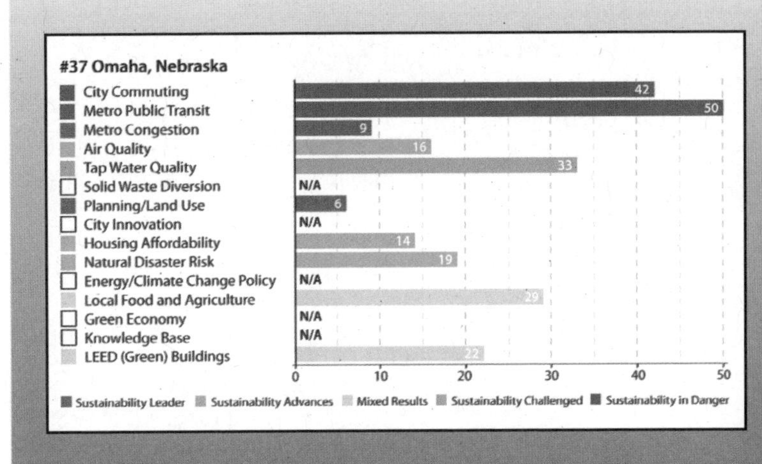

Healthy Living

Omaha's water ranks #33, with 26 contaminants, 4 of which exceed the EPA's recommended limits, but its air isn't so bad at #16. The city has plenty of parks, covering 11 percent of the city area, including 80 miles of trails. The city ranks #29 in food and agriculture with a farmers' market downtown that offers local produce, crafts and meat. The Buy Fresh, Buy Local campaign connects Nebraskans to local farmers, helping to build a sense of community around local food producers.

Getting Around

Though Omaha is not nearly as sprawling as most cities in our study, you do need a car to get around easily. The city's Metro Area Transit takes less than 2 percent of the city's residents to work each day, with 81 percent of commuters driving alone. Two key advocacy, education and planning groups, Omaha by Design and the Joslyn Castle Institute, are actively promoting green solutions for the city, including more bicycle paths and trails, healthy lifestyles and urban revitalization, such as mixed-use development that reduces reliance on cars.

The Omaha Public Power District derives 10 megawatts of energy from renewable sources, including a wind turbine generator and landfill gas-to-energy plant.

Economic Factors

Omaha's economy isn't currently very green, but there are visions for making it greener. The revitalization of downtown has been a good first step. The current plan embraced by the mayor and Planning Department aspires to bring together public and private investment and philanthropic contributions focusing on landscape, environment, design guidelines, public art, building preservation, and the creation of new, walkable neighborhoods as the city grows.

The Joslyn Castle Institute is trying to establish the Nebraska Center for Sustainable Construction to support deconstruction and salvage as an alternative to demolition. Omaha ranks #22 for green building; the National Park Service Midwest Regional Headquarters was the first LEED Certified project in Nebraska.

The Omaha Public Power District derives 10 megawatts of energy from renewable sources, including a wind turbine generator and landfill gas-to-energy plant. (Omaha was not officially ranked in energy because city government officials did not complete our survey.)

Summary/Next Steps

Omaha has some programs that promise to accelerate its efforts to become more sustainable. Omaha's urban revitalization, commitment to park space, and recent expansion of renewable energy reveal its focus on creating a healthier environment for its citizens — right in line with its pragmatic Midwestern values.

The city has reportedly been rewriting building guidelines to incorporate the recommendations of Omaha by Design, another positive sign for residents. Continuing to support renewable energy and creating more public transit options — perhaps with light rail — could help catapult the city upward in future rankings.

38

Atlanta, Georgia

Inland Port Takes Baby Steps

Atlanta gets high marks for green building — indeed, it's a national showcase for sustainable architecture — but in most other areas it appears burdened with industrial consequences.

Atlanta's airport is the busiest in the world. Founded as a rail terminus — its first name was Terminus — the city has always been important to transit and industry. When Union forces marched on Atlanta in 1864, they were attacking the logistics hub of the Confederate Army. Today, Atlanta is a foreign trade zone — imports can speed directly from the coast to US Customs in Atlanta. More freight than ever converges on the rail center of the South, where goods are sorted, re-sorted, and sent along to oceans and skies beyond.

Thanks in part to the 1996 Olympic Games, Atlanta's commercial identity has prospered along with its importance as a waypoint in the global economy. People continue to move here in droves: Atlanta metro has the fastest-growing sprawl in the nation.

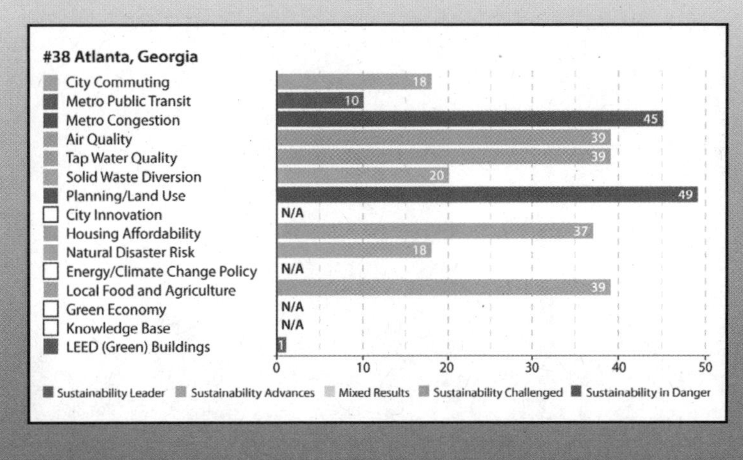

Healthy Living

All of the coming and going takes its toll on the city's air. The power plants firing coal for the grid and vehicles idling in traffic contribute to the city's low air-quality ranking (#39). Atlanta is among the lowest-ranked cities nationwide in terms of particulate pollution (soot), and it also has ample ozone pollution (smog).

That's not news to anyone in the area who drives to work through the haze. Emergency rooms see a spike in asthma cases during the summer smog season. In recent years, since the EPA downgraded the air pollution in Atlanta from "serious" to "severe," the city has improved its air quality slightly. The city's tap water ranks #39.

Sprawl induced traffic and air quality problems are endemic to the Atlanta metro region.

Wikipedia / GNU FDL1.2

Atlanta has been slow to develop local food networks. There is some general demand for organics — Whole Foods has landed at several locations in Atlanta — but community-supported agriculture and farmers' markets are scarce, and the city ranks #39 in overall local food and agriculture. It also scores low in terms of parkland, with less than 4 percent of the city devoted to recreational green space.

Getting Around

Traffic in Atlanta is average for an American city. Long hauls to and from the surrounding metro area are reportedly more affected than movement within the city. Over 12 percent of citizens use the subway and buses run by the city, which places Atlanta ahead of the curve for public transit (#10). What's more, the buses run on compressed natural gas. But there's minimal push for a comprehensive transit system that reshapes land use. Most plans to enhance public transit focus on building up the commuter rail service using existing freight railroad lines.

Economic Factors

Atlanta is embracing clean technologies at street level, with more LEED Certified buildings than anywhere else in the South. Atlanta ranks first in terms of green building initiatives. The city boasts the first Gold-certified LEED building in the Southeast and is on track to enjoy bragging rights for the region's first Platinum certification. A cluster of LEED buildings is going up in midtown Atlanta. One of those buildings houses a Georgia Tech business school program and has garnered praise from the US Green Building Council.

Some of the expansions underway at Atlanta's world-class airport will reflect green building techniques inspired by LEED. In fact, Atlanta requires all new and renovated city-funded structures over a certain size or cost to rate at least silver on the LEED scale. The Green Building Council, which authors the LEED standards, held its last annual conference here. Take a bow, Atlanta.

Summary/Next Steps

The city's excellence in green building suggests a willingness to confront long-term environmental issues, but the modest motto of Atlanta's Energy Conservation Program, "A step towards sustainability," is all too accurate. Atlanta would benefit by planning more boldly to translate its current economic dynamism into a durable, vital metropolitan center — one that not only thrives on the worldwide circulation of commodities, but also addresses the vulnerabilities caused by runaway sprawl.

Atlanta is already rife with ideas for sustainability, with nonprofits shouldering a lot of the work. Southface Energy, for instance, promotes sustainable building practices. It runs a resource center in midtown Atlanta and has collaborated with Oak Ridge National Laboratory to showcase renewable energy and energy conservation technologies for homeowners.

Such forward thinking could play a greater role in city planning and development. Instead of reacting piecemeal to environmental and health issues as they arise, Atlanta has an opportunity to confront sustainability with the same tenacity with which it positioned itself as a leader in the turbulent global shipping industry.

Atlanta is embracing clean technologies at street level, with more LEED Certified buildings than anywhere else in the South.

39

Houston, Texas

Moving Forward

In SustainLane's 2005 US City Rankings, which benchmarked 25 cities, Houston came in last place. Citizens' meetings, Internet bulletin boards and local radio talk shows were full of reactions to our analysis — many of them negative, all of them impassioned. Locals said there were things going on in sustainability and environmental management that we failed to acknowledge.

Part of the problem was that the city didn't have anyone in place to manage, measure or communicate sustainability performance. Since our rankings came out in June 2005, Mayor Bill White appointed a Director of Environmental Programming to work across the city's departments so Houstonians and others can find out what's happening more easily. The city has also made some positive steps toward a more sustainable future.

The public outcry and reaction to our study demonstrate that the city cares about building a better future for its residents. Houston ranks #39 out of 50 cities this year. Up-and-coming green projects, elements of a clean tech incubator, and affordable housing all augur a positive direction for the nation's fourth largest city.

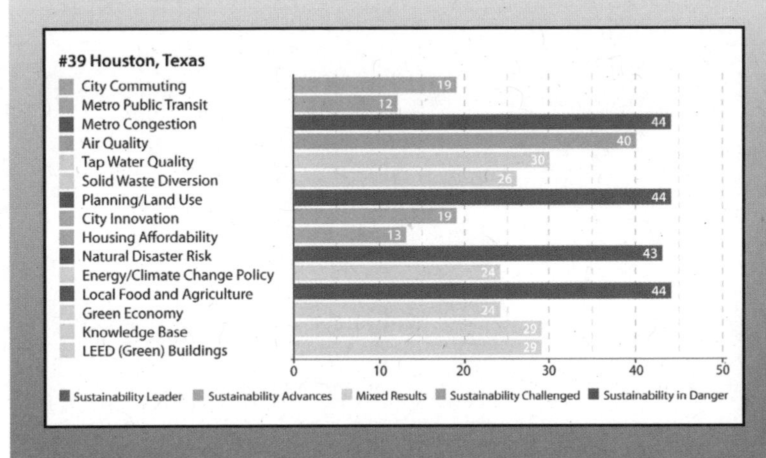

Healthy Living

Air quality is a problem (#40), with a Clean Air Act violation in ozone and a low overall day-to-day air quality index rating — consider checking out the EPA's air quality forecast for Houston before going out to play.

Water quality is also below par (#30), with 19 contaminants found, 4 of which are over the recommended limit.

In terms of local food and agriculture, the city ranks #44, with only two farmers' markets and 70 community gardens — unfortunate tallies for a city of about 2 million with a year-round growing climate. Parks are not so easy to come by, either. Only 5.7 percent of Houston is covered in parkland, putting it in the bottom third of the 50 cities in our study.

As previously mentioned, the city has shown a commitment to strengthening its sustainability performance by appointing a Director of Environmental Programming.

Getting Around

Houston's public transit ridership dropped near the watershed 5 percent point in 2004 — once it falls below that point, people tend to forget that public transit is even an option. City voters passed Metro Solutions in 2004, which will provide funds for a long-range build-out of commuter rail, light rail and better bus service. As of mid-2006, the added transit systems were in the late planning stages. With over 75 percent of Houstonians driving alone to work, and under 2 percent walking or biking to work, Metro Solutions comes not a moment too soon.

Economic Factors

A fossil fuel energy boomtown, Houston also performs relatively well in sustainability-related economic ventures. The city gets about 2 percent of its energy from renewable sources, and features a clean technology testing center aimed at developing low-sulfur diesel in conjunction with the University of Texas. In developing such a clean tech venture, the city not only creates jobs in a next-generation industry, it will also be able to apply the technology in its own market, potentially helping to ease air pollution problems.

Houston has very affordable housing (#13), but that doesn't stop developers and home buyers from pushing beyond its sprawled outer limits, where new gated developments continue to gobble up everything from pine forests to wetlands.

Green buildings are on the rise (#29) as the city attempts to reconcile its helter-skelter development approaches — no zoning, little transit-oriented development — with sustainable building practices.

Natural disaster risk (#43) is a serious issue for Houston, and the adjacent Gulf of Mexico that spawned close-call Hurricane Rita in 2005 is forecast to be active over the coming 10-20 year cycle.

Summary/Next Steps

International fossil fuel energy companies experienced windfall profits in 2006. The question is how much of the economic success of these global companies will trickle down to improve overall quality of life in Houston, especially for lower-income residents and for those who work in industries that aren't reaping extraordinary earnings. As previously mentioned, the city has shown a commitment to strengthening its sustainability performance by appointing a Director of Environmental Programming. Improving air quality, reducing roadway congestion (#44), and creating sources for local food are all opportunities to positively affect the quality of life for residents throughout Houston.

40

Tulsa, Oklahoma

Rich History. Clean Tech Future?

Originally a cattle town in the 1880s, Tulsa was irrevocably changed in 1901 when the first oil gusher was struck in Spindletop, Texas. The wealth that the oil industry generated in both Texas and Oklahoma guaranteed a rapid cultural and developmental transformation for the entire region.

By the 1920s, "T-Town," as musicians referred to it, was a hotbed of jazz and blues. The art deco buildings that still dot the Tulsa landscape were part of the 1920s building boom. The city continued to thrive until the oil bust of the early 1980s. Tulsa is now once again an important fossil fuel energy center with very little commitment to less cyclical, more sustainable living. There are some noteworthy community-based projects for locally produced food, but Tulsa has virtually no public transportation and remains an auto-dependent US city.

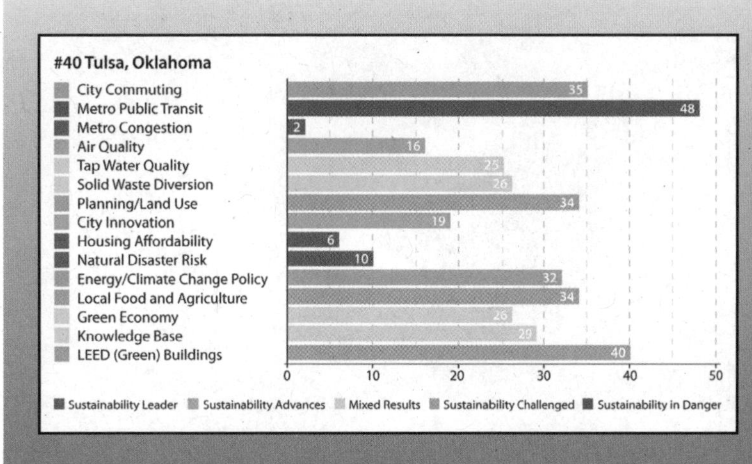

Healthy Living

Parks lining the Arkansas River are popular destinations for hiking, fishing, kayaking, biking and more. Despite this pleasant byway, Tulsa ranks #32 for its city park acreage as a percentage of total city land.

Several municipal and nonprofit groups are working to improve both air and drinking water quality. Tulsa ranks #25 in tap water quality and #16 in air quality. The city's Partners for a Clean Environment program aims to reduce the use of hazardous materials that pollute Tulsa's water, land and air.

Tulsa has only two official farmers' markets and seven community gardens, placing the city #34 in local food and agriculture. One unique food cooperative, however, provides locally grown food to cities throughout Oklahoma. The Oklahoma Food Cooperative distributes locally made, often-organic goods to cities throughout Oklahoma. The

"The Golden Driller, a symbol of the International Petroleum Exposition. Dedicated to the men of the petroleum industry who by their vision and daring have created from God's abundance a better life for mankind." –inscription

DON SIBLEY

organization is now helping people throughout the region start locally grown food co-ops in their own communities.

Getting Around

Tulsa ranks #35 in commuting and #48 in public transportation. Only 1.5 percent of the population commutes to work on public transit. Almost four out of five residents drive to work alone. Carshare and carpool programs help account for at least some of the significant number of people (11 percent) who carpool to work. None of the city fleet vehicles use alternative fuels.

Many other cities in this study have low public transit ridership. However, most of those cities have realized the importance of reversing that trend and are in the process of planning and implementing public transit alternatives. Considering that the nation may be facing higher gas prices and significant gas supply issues over the next years, Tulsa could benefit from investigating what those other cities are doing.

Economic Factors

Tulsa has a large city footprint composed of communities with a lot of personality, from art deco downtown buildings to the jazzy Greenwood Historical District, to the affluent South Tulsa. Many of the older neighborhoods have been rehabilitated, and downtown is thriving. Although its reputation as an oil king is just a memory, other industry continues to thrive. Tulsa is an important business center, with aerospace, telecom, high tech and insurance. While the city core does seem to be growing, there's little action around sustainable development approaches.

Tulsa is notable in that it has one of the only city-affiliated clean tech incubators in the nation. The private, not-for-profit incubator i2E helps homegrown technology companies get started and grow. In this way, i2E creates jobs and renewable-energy or energy-efficient technologies that may be used in Tulsa. Two Tulsa-based companies involved in this partnership are Excel Energy and LuXsine. Excel Energy's technology system monitors and helps users program and more effectively limit energy consumption 24 hours a day, every day of the year. LuXsine aims to dramatically enhance solar energy efficiencies.

Meanwhile, Tulsa Area Clean Cities is trying to bring renewable and sustainable energy to Tulsa in an effort to increase local economic opportunity and reduce oil dependency.

Summary/Next Steps

Like other lower-ranking cities with very little infrastructure or planning for sustainable living, Tulsa has a lot of work to do. What sets Tulsa

Rowers on the Arkansas River in downtown Tulsa.

Don Sibley

apart from those cities is that it has both for-profit and nonprofit groups that promote renewable energy. The city would do well to tap into some of these local project innovators and make their important work more accessible to the larger community.

Overall, Tulsa has a lot of opportunities to become more sustainable. It might consider public transportation, green building incentives for commercial or residential building, creating an environmental department, and developing a sustainability plan. Each of these mutually supportive elements could help support better livability while reducing the economy's vulnerability.

41

Arlington, Texas

City at a Crossroads

Arlington's come a long way since being founded in 1875 as a railroad stop between its larger neighbors Dallas and Fort Worth. It could use some rails today as it faces the challenges of growing a public transportation infrastructure and the consequences of automobile-induced sprawl development. Fortunately, Arlington leaders and members of the community have already started to plan: In its 2025 Vision Plan, which identifies several key areas for improvement, the need to improve mobility made the shortlist, as did reducing poverty, reversing declining home values and preventing the loss of retail dollars to surrounding communities.

Healthy Living

The city boasts high scores in water quality (#10) and housing affordability (#6). Despite heavy automobile dependence, air quality is above average (#22), though road congestion (#40) is some of the nation's worst. The city has recognized the need to make more pedestrian and bike-friendly neighborhoods. Arlington has taken an initial step in developing local food resources — the city recently held a dedication ceremony for its first community garden. Arlington has no farmers' markets.

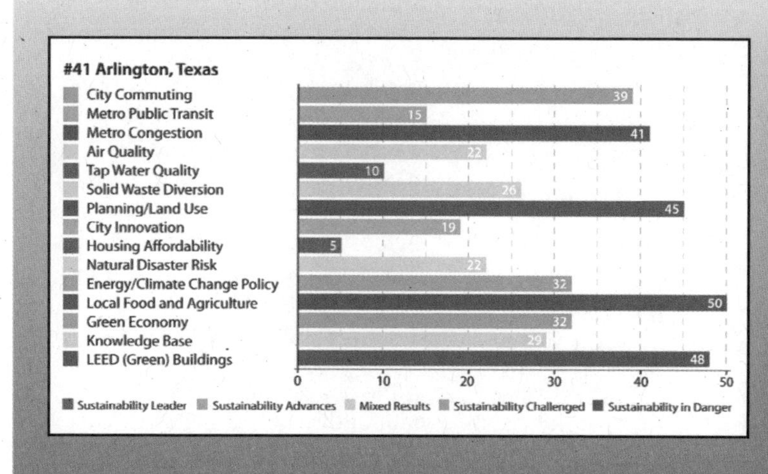

Getting Around

Since the last trolley ride in 1934, Arlington has gone without a public transportation system. Not surprisingly, it ranks last in commuters' use of public transportation. (Its ranking at #15 for regional public transportation is a result of being in the Dallas metro region.) Complete automobile dependence has led to significant sprawl, yet citizens have twice voted down public transit ballot funding measures, most recently in 2002.

However, residents now seem to be having second thoughts. One of the goals in the city's 2025 Vision

Plan is to comprehensively address mobility needs through participation in the development of a regional, multi-modal transportation network.

There have been increased calls for speeding up the conversion of existing freight lines to passenger rail service connecting Dallas, Arlington and Fort Worth.

creating incentives for building green would help Arlington make "significant progress toward reducing waste, energy consumption and water consumption.

Economic Factors

Arlington ranks below average in green economic development, with no clean tech incubation program and low scores in green building (#48) and local food and agriculture (#50). The city ranks #22 for natural disaster risk, though it has weathered its share of troubles over time, including super tornadoes, flash floods and severe hail and thunderstorms. Having reached out to Hurricane Katrina survivors, Arlington residents are well aware of the chaos and suffering that a natural disaster can cause. The city's Office of Emergency Management is taking steps to prepare for disaster by educating the public about natural disaster risks along with coordinating the city's response to disaster.

Summary/Next Steps

Unlike most cities we studied, Arlington still has undeveloped land. The city might consider turning some of that land into parks — its ratio of city land to parks is slightly below average. Where it does develop land, creating incentives for building green would help Arlington make significant progress toward reducing waste, energy consumption and water consumption while promoting healthy regional economic development. Piggybacking on The University of Texas at Arlington's business incubator would be the perfect way to support local clean tech businesses aimed at the emerging green building, water purification and renewable energy markets. Mixed-use and higher density developments would be another compelling way to help get residents out of their cars and into local businesses.

42

Nashville, Tennessee

Music City

Along with the rest of Tennessee, Nashville (population 550,000) experienced a migration boom last decade. A dynamic national economy meant more jobs in many counties of Tennessee, which in turn created one of the fastest growth rates in the country. People came, lured by good jobs and mild seasons. Housing and services expanded to absorb the influx. The boom is now mostly over. The settlers of the 1990s are entrenched in their suburban enclaves, the subdivisions no longer brand-new.

Businesses came to Nashville, too. Major health care corporations made the city their regional base, and Nissan North America is now headquartered here. The city remains an attractive place for businesses to relocate, helped by its vibrant music scene, quality workforce and positive business climate.

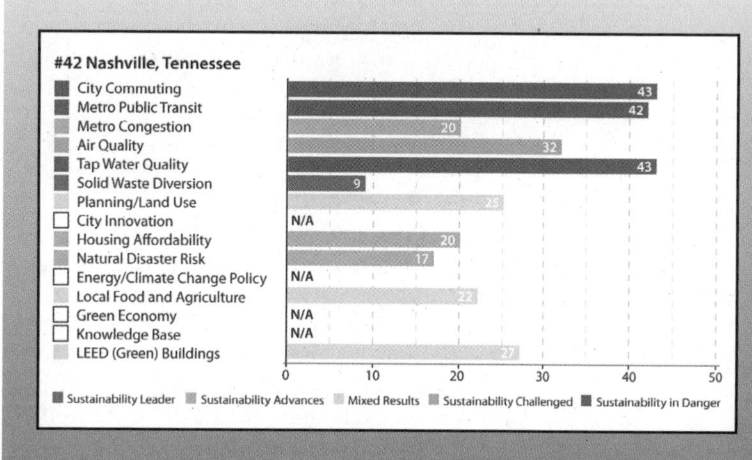

Healthy Living

Human-made and natural emissions mix to result in air quality that ranks #32 in our study. City tap water ranks at #43, with 23 contaminants, 6 of which exceed recommended limits. Green space within the city is minimal, as the city provisions only 3.2 percent of its overall land use for greenbelts and parks, one of the lower scores in our study (#48).

The city boasts a historic public market dating back to 1828, where customers can find fresh, local goods. Community Supported Agriculture is also available to Nashville in small numbers. The city ranks #22 for local foods indicators, in the middle of the pack.

Getting Around

The heart of Nashville is surrounded by sprawl. Traffic congestion within the metro area, ranking #20 in our study, is not too bad; most commuting is done between suburbs. But

Nashville ranks #9 for waste diversion, an excellent score for a city where recycling is not mandated by law.

nearly 81 percent of residents drive alone to work, while only 2 percent take public transit.

Efforts to counter sprawl are underway. A nonprofit consortium of planners and architects called the Civic Design Center provides one of the most innovative and comprehensive plans for centering the urban core of Nashville. Its design philosophy emphasizes community integrity and public transit so that the city emerges with character and cohesion, even as sprawl continues to exert its outward pressure. The resulting Plan of Nashville is worth checking out.

Economic Factors

The city ranks #9 for waste diversion, an excellent score for a city where recycling is not mandated by law. Most successful is a citywide curbside program, Curby, which currently has upwards of 50 percent of households binning mixed paper, cardboard and aluminum cans alongside normal garbage. Meanwhile, a nonprofit called Bring Urban Recycling to Nashville Today (BURNT) advocates a far more comprehensive recycling strategy that includes composting organic waste.

In green buildings per capita, Nashville ranks #27, with six LEED Registered buildings and one LEED Certified structure. Renewable energy projects and economic development are not on the city's front burner, though the Adventure Science Center does feature a solar array that was installed in conjunction with the Tennessee Valley Authority.

Summary/Next Steps

Nashville has been slow to adopt an articulated sustainability regime, but the Plan of Nashville presents a compelling course that could help mitigate long commute times and worsening air quality. As in many cities, small groups of citizens and professionals here are offering exceptional, often inspired, solutions to local problems. If city government can take the reins and channel this energy, using its successes in areas such as solid waste management as a model, Nashville has an opportunity to move rapidly toward a more sustainable future.

43

Detroit, Michigan

Opportunities for Change

The automotive industry has pervaded Detroit life for more than 50 years. When the Big Three automakers — Ford, General Motors and Chrysler — have experienced good times, so have the people of Detroit. Since 1998, however, Chrysler has been owned by German automaker Daimler-Benz, and Ford and General Motors have struggled to compete with Japanese carmakers.

Meanwhile, Detroit is losing population to outlying areas and other states. It lost about 50,000 of its citizens between 2000 and 2004, after shedding about half of its population from 1950 to 2000. Detroit is the poorest large city in the nation, with unemployment around 15 percent as of late 2005, and more than a third of its residents living below the poverty line. With a mindset looking forward, the city has an excellent opportunity to take advantage of emerging clean technologies, including alternative fuels and advanced transportation technologies, and regain its prominence as a design and engineering heavyweight.

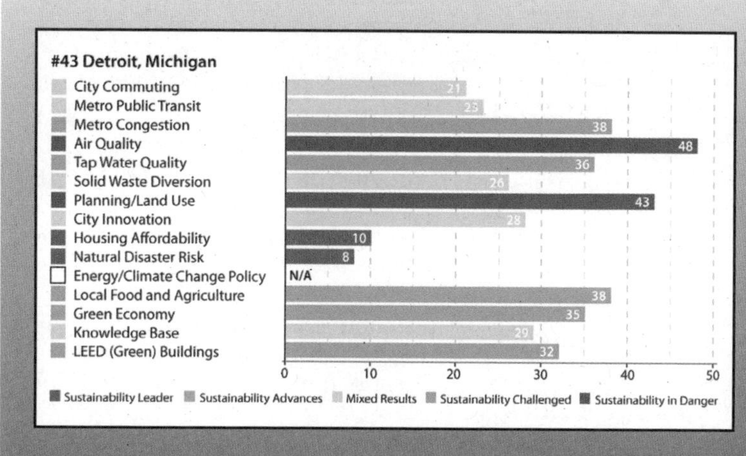

Healthy Living

Air quality is a constant challenge (#48), with year-round particle pollution from soot. Ozone pollution is also "marginal" according to the EPA. Tap water, originating from nearby Lake St. Clair, ranks below average at #36 with 18 contaminants, 5 of which exceed the EPA's recommended limits.

Park space is slightly below average at #28, taking up 6.6 percent of total acreage. Belle Island is the largest island park in a US city, and other parks include the 1,100-acre Rogue Park, which is the city's largest.

Local food overall ranks #38, with one of the nation's lower rates of farmers' markets per capita. The city does have 43 community gardens, however. The Detroit Garden Resource Project is an innovative nonprofit that provides resources and information to help residents, schools and communities grow their own food.

Getting Around

Though Detroit is dependent on the automotive industry for its economy, city leaders have shown some foresight in providing alternatives for public transportation. The city ranks #21 in commute-to-work practices: 7.5 percent of Detroiters ride public transit to work, though less than 3 percent bike or walk. Another 11 percent carpool, leaving about 76 percent who drive to work alone. The surrounding metro area ranks #23 for overall transit ridership. Roadways aren't always smooth sailing for cars or bus public transit, as the city ranks #38 in metro area street and freeway congestion.

The Detroit Garden Resource Project is an innovative nonprofit that provides resources and information to help residents, schools and communities grow their own food.

Economic Factors

Detroit automakers are trying to catch up to Toyota after the success of its Prius and higher gas prices signaled a change for the industry. Ford is ramping up production of hybrid car and passenger truck lines, while GM is staking its research and development on fuel cells and "flex fuel" engines that run on a mix of ethanol and unleaded gasoline.

Both companies, however, face an uphill battle to regain their market dominance. Ford has made a significant investment in green building. Its River Rouge Plant, completed in 2005, features a large green rooftop, rainwater run-off purification, and indoor daylighting. On the whole, Detroit ranks #32 in green building.

There are certainly reasons for optimism. A state of Michigan nonprofit based at Detroit's Wayne State University, NextEnergy, was established to help automakers and suppliers commercialize alternative fuel technologies. And Detroit rates well in both housing affordability, at #10, and natural disaster risk, at #8.

Summary/Next Steps

If Detroit could harness its old-school transportation supply and labor base with alternative-fuel technologies and products, it would possess a ready-made migration path into the future. The city has no shortage of brilliant engineers, marketers and mechanics to draw upon.

GM announced in November 2006 that it would be going into production "at a later date" with a plug-in hybrid SUV, called the Saturn Vue Green, that would get twice the mileage of previous models. When the model would hit the market was not available.

The US automotive industry has been slow to embrace change, instead choosing to lobby Congress against raising the nation's fuel efficiency standards. Large vehicles with high-powered engines have ruled the day in Detroit, but with higher gas prices, they don't appear to have a bright future. By investing in renewable energy, alternative fuel, local food and green building, Detroit stands to improve the lives of its residents — and keep more of them in town.

43

Memphis, Tennessee

Living for Today

For many of Memphis's million annual visitors, Elvis's Graceland or Sun Studios are the main attractions. Few realize that Memphis is the South's largest city outside of Florida and an important symbol of the Civil Rights Movement.

Located on the fertile bluffs of the Mississippi, Memphis used to be an economic and military center. After the Civil War, Memphis became a mecca for freed slaves. When a yellow fever epidemic wiped out nearly a quarter of the population, Memphis responded by building the most advanced sewage treatment facility of the time, and by locating a new water source: the legendary Artesian Springs. It is this ability to rebound from strife and tragedy — more recently Martin Luther King's assassination at a local motel — that has made Memphis the great city it is today. However, little progress has been made in ensuring the city's long-term future.

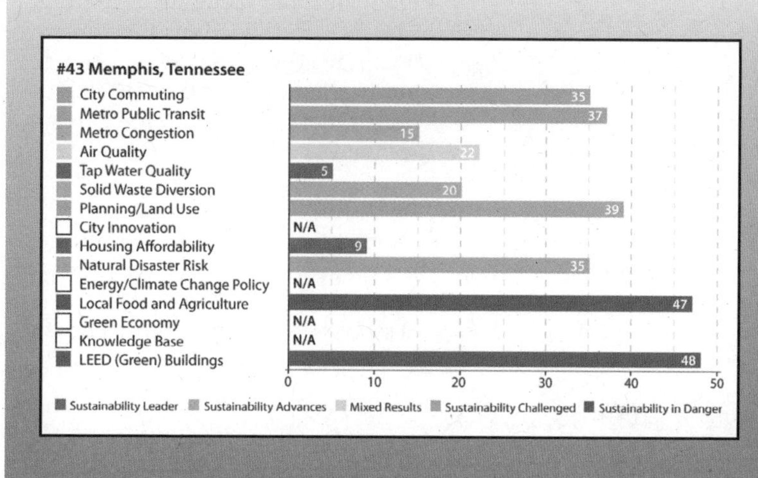

Healthy Living

Memphians are blessed with clean water (ranked #5 in our study), above-average air (#22), and a graceful system of parks that cater to children and families. The city plans to revitalize the park system by developing a greenway to encircle the city and refurbishing its historical parkways.

Besides its legendary barbeque, Memphis has a dearth of local food. Despite a favorable growing climate, local produce is hard to find; the city has only one farmers' market and one community garden, where a few souls at the Mid-South Peace and Justice Center are doing their part to bring healthy, homegrown food to residents.

Getting Around

Memphis prides itself on being a regional transportation hub. But the average citizen who needs to get from point A to point B usually does so in a car. Commuters rely almost exclusively on the automobile — over 81 percent drive alone to work. Another 12 percent carpool, leaving a smattering of walkers and public transportation riders.

As for public transportation, the city has invested in retooling its original trolley system in the downtown area and along the riverfront. This has been good for tourism and downtown business development but has had little impact on the transportation habits of the average resident.

Economic Factors

Memphis's Chamber of Commerce has waged a 20-year campaign to declare Memphis "America's Distribution Center." FedEx and two other Fortune 500 companies have located here, along with a diverse range of other businesses such as agribusiness, retail, tourism and even filmmaking. State fiscal policies favor business development — there is no state income or payroll tax, and a "right to work" policy allows workers to be hired without union membership.

Housing is affordable here. The cost of the average house was among the least expensive of any city we analyzed, just under $85,000, which puts Memphis at #9 for affordability when considering average incomes.

Main Street trolley on recently redeveloped downtown system.

Jeremy Atherton / CreativeCommons 2.5

Summary/Next Steps

Memphis is a proud city with strong cultural traditions and an efficient, well-run government. Nonetheless, it lacks leadership and management for city sustainability issues. Mpact Memphis is trying to improve Memphis by inspiring the under-40 generation to make their city a better place. With clean water and decent air, city officials and residents have terrific strengths to work from in building a more sustainable public transportation infrastructure and economy.

45

Indianapolis, Indiana

Time for a Pit Stop?

Indianapolis is a city with a long automotive history extending well beyond Formula One racecars. It's no surprise, then, that the city has a car-based culture. There are few public transportation alternatives. Natural gas was discovered in Indianapolis in the 1890s. The city offered free gas to companies that were built there, which led to a booming local automobile industry at the turn of the 20th century. (The Indianapolis 500 began during this era.) Although the boom ended in 1915 when local natural gas ran out, the automobile continued to play an important role in the city's economic history.

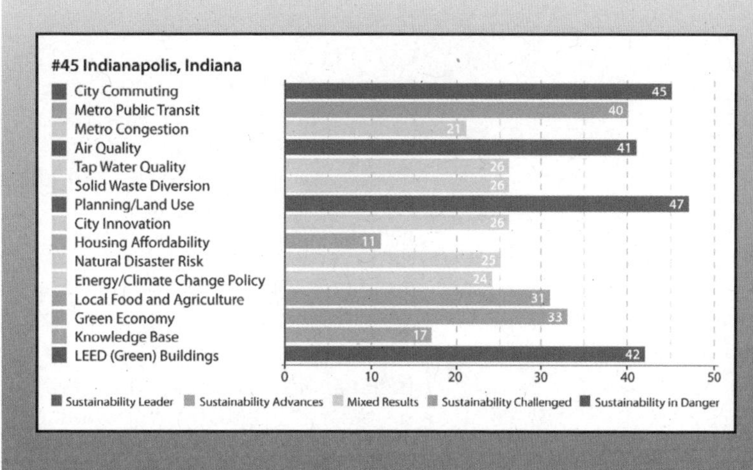

Today, four interstates intersect in Indianapolis, make it a major trucking center and a regional transportation hub connecting Chicago, Louisville, Cincinnati, Columbus, St. Louis and other cities. The extensive network of highways has allowed Indianapolis to enjoy a relatively low amount of traffic congestion for a city of its size.

Healthy Living

Though surrounded by crops, mostly soybean and cornfields, Indianapolis has only five farmers' markets and ranks #31 for overall local food and agriculture. The Marion Cooperative Extension does offer urban garden classes and recently catalogued 74 community gardens.

Several parks and trails weave their way through the city — the city ranks #39 in percent of city land devoted to parks. The long-defunct Central Canal was recently refurbished and reopened as a city recreational area with pedal boats, jogging and bicycle paths that snake through downtown. Eagle Creek Park, purported to be the fourth-largest city-owned park in the country, was a result of the grassroots efforts of local citizens. You can now enjoy 1,400 acres for sailing, rowing and swimming, plus 3,900 acres for landlubber activities.

The Monon Trail is a greenway that winds through the center of the north side of Indianapolis, linking commercial districts, neighborhoods and parks. On warm weekends, users are often shoulder-to-shoulder jogging, walking and hiking.

Air quality in Indianapolis ranks quite low (#41), one area that the city is taking action to address. The city plans to plant 100,000 trees over the next ten years, and has established internal policies like flexible workday schedules and idle-reduction policies for all city vehicles. The city has a significant number of alternative-fueled vehicles, with 12.5 percent of the fleet using lower-emission fuels.

The city plans to plant 100,000 trees over the next ten years, and has established internal policies like flexible workday schedules and idle-reduction policies for all city vehicles.

Unlike many other cities, Indianapolis is blessed with a water source that originates within the city limits. Unfortunately, the quality of tap water isn't great (#26), with 13 contaminants, including 4 over the recommended EPA limit.

Getting Around

Ranked #45 in commute-to-work practices, most of the residents (83 percent) drive to work in their car alone. Less than 2 percent use public transportation. Despite the abundance of greenways connecting neighborhoods within the city, only 1 percent walk to work and almost no one rides a bicycle to work. Perhaps a testament to the city's carpool program, 10 percent of residents carpool to work. A carshare program does not presently exist, though you can sign up for a commuter match list at Central Indiana Commuter Services.

A public transportation plan based on transit between downtown and the suburbs was recently halted because federal funding fell through. The plan included buses on dedicated lines, light rail trolley and elevated monorail. Many city officials and residents are pushing to continue with the plan without the federal funds. While this is evidence of a community concerned with improving its deficient public transit, the city really needs funding, increased community awareness, and dedication to make it a reality.

Economic Factors

Local government, businesses, and universities in Indiana are demonstrating interest in and commitment to renewable energy. Since the state is a leading producer of soybeans and corn, it's a logical step to encourage the production of fuel from those sources. In fact, the state has made a commitment to increase biofuels, including biodiesel.

BioCrossroads, a coalition that includes locally headquartered pharmaceuticals giant Eli Lilly, the city of Indianapolis, Purdue University, and others, is seeking ways to grow Indiana's clean-tech economy. In a 2004 study, the group developed a strategy to increase economic growth through agriculture. The plan calls for increased production of biofuels based on grain and oilseed, helping farmers' find niches for their produce, and the incubation of innovative food programs that use Indiana commodities for nutritious and healthy food.

Summary/Next Steps

Indianapolis has a great opportunity to begin moving from a fossil fuel economy to more sustainable modes of living, and to cultivate industries around biofuels. While it is a hub of a larger interstate highway network, the city stands to benefit by expanding its bus service and providing more public transit options for its expansive suburbs. As oil prices increase, such tactics will provide options and economic relief to area residents.

The city can help improve its energy security by initiating a sustainability plan and by offering commercial and residential green building incentives. Public awareness and participation in planning and prioritizing all of these issues will be important for any type of sustainability initiatives led by local government.

Aerial view of downtown Indianapolis including dominant interstate system.

DEREK JENSEN / PUBLIC DOMAIN

46

Fort Worth, Texas

Taking Steps Toward Sustainability

Founded as a military camp in 1849, Fort Worth earned the nickname "Cowtown" because of its central role in the cattle drives and ranching business of the 19th century. The opening of the railroad in 1876 cemented its status as the hub of the Texas stockyards. When oil was discovered in West Texas early in the 20th century, Fort Worth's strategic location on the railroad helped it become a nexus of the oil business.

Fort Worth has come a long way from its dusty beginnings as a stop on the Chisholm Trail. It now boasts major cultural destinations such as art museums, a symphony, opera and a ballet company. Fort Worth celebrates its ranching heritage throughout the year; the National Cowgirl Museum tips its hat to women's contributions to Cowtown's vibrant history.

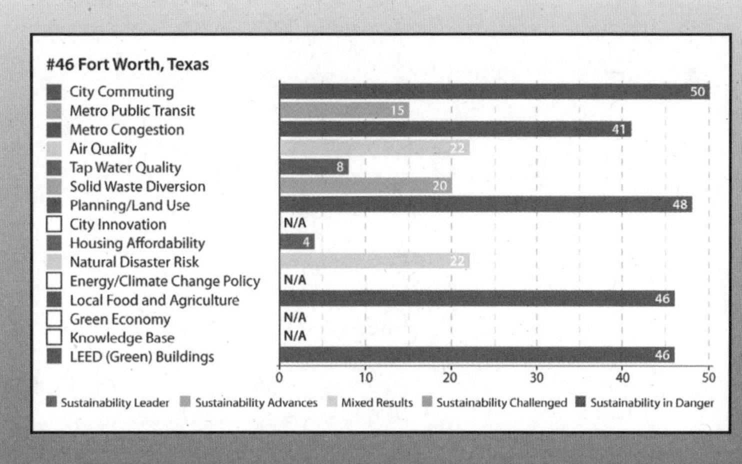

Healthy Living

People here are fortunate to have clean water (#8) and the elegant Trinity River, with its 35 miles of pedestrian trails. Although Fort Worth has a relatively low percentage of open space compared to other cities in the study, 75 percent of residents report using their parks for hiking, walking and playing.

Fort Worth is behind the curve when it comes to local food resources, ranking #46. Despite a long growing season, it has only two farmers' markets. School children in at least one elementary school gardening program are, however, getting their hands dirty. City leaders might consider developing a local food supply. Community gardens, for instance, would provide residents with a greater sense of community and a more secure food supply while promoting project-based education.

Getting Around

Fort Worth is making a concerted effort to reduce air pollution caused

Fort Worth is also working to improve its bicycling commute options by providing lockers and equipping all transit vehicles with bike racks.

by automobile traffic through a variety of incentives, including free transit passes and comp time for city workers who carpool. The programs have helped to dramatically increase the number of city employees who use public transit or carpool. Fort Worth is also working to improve its bicycling commute options by providing lockers and equipping all transit vehicles with bike racks. Those are encouraging signs, but Fort Worth ranks near last in our commuting category, with nearly 85 percent of residents driving alone to work.

Fort Worth has launched a number of initiatives to encourage a move away from suburban sprawl development. Neighborhood Empowerment Zones promote compact urban villages located close to transit, enabling people to walk to basic services and promoting a sense of community. Fort Worth also offers a Smart Commute mortgage homebuyer program for residents who choose to live close to transit services.

Economic Factors

Fort Worth's historical economy of ranching, agriculture and petroleum extraction was based on using the land's resources. While remnants of that heritage remain, the economic sectors most important to today's Fort Worth economy include aviation, logistics, defense, technology and transportation. Leaders in a few of those industries are starting to build green, notably Radio Shack, which is seeking LEED certification for its new headquarters on the banks of the Trinity River. It would be encouraging to see more businesses follow that example — the city ranks #46 in green building.

Summary/Next Steps

Fort Worth has identified better land use, air quality, solid waste reduction, storm water management and energy conservation as important targets for improving the environment, and has even been named one of America's Most Livable Communities. To help it remain livable in the long run, Fort Worth might consider investing in sustainability efforts. Texas cities Austin, San Antonio and Dallas all have programs that can serve as models.

Fort Worth is more dependent on the automobile than most US cities. The good news is that it has a relatively strong public transportation system (#15) and is taking concrete action to increase the number of people who commute to work. Developing a local food supply and renewable energy sources, and continuing to support transit-oriented development would be good steps toward improving its overall ranking.

47

Mesa, Arizona

Surviving the Desert Boom

Most people would never guess that Mesa has more residents than household-name cities like Miami, Minneapolis, and Honolulu. Nor would most venture that Mesa is home to more Mormons than any other city (it was founded by a Mormon leader in 1877).

Unfortunately, the city gets low marks across most of the sustainability categories we analyzed: #32 in commuting, #35 in planning, and #34 in tap water quality. Mesa's sprawled, suburban character results from a bedroom-community existence — there's no historically defined city center and the town lacks urban planning approaches that other fast-growing cities are finding necessary to cope with their challenges.

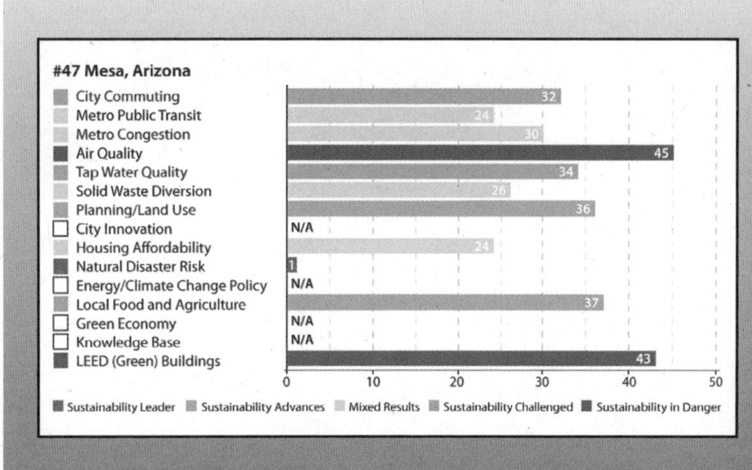

Healthy Living

With dry desert air and expansive views of the Superstition Mountains (on clear days), Mesa would be perfect for an active outdoor lifestyle, if not for its sketchy air quality (#45). The city's air is in violation of the EPA's Clean Air Act for ozone, and in "serious" violation for large particulate matter. Residents should take care to check air quality conditions before exercising outdoors.

About 3.6 percent of Mesa's land is used for parks, which puts it at #46 in our study. Local food ranks #37 overall, with three farmers' markets in the city. Mesa had 1 community garden we could locate in our survey. The tap water contains 16 contaminants, including 3 that exceed the EPA's recommended threshold (#34).

Getting Around

Like other Sunbelt boomtowns, Mesa is almost completely dependent on automotive transportation: Almost 79 percent of Mesa's residents drive to work alone. Public transit commute ridership is about 1 percent, one of the lowest rates in our study. The city's metro bus service operates only six days a week. Biking and walking together make up about 3 percent of commuter trips. Carpooling is the one bright spot, with an above-average 12 percent of commuters sharing a ride to work.

Carpooling is the one bright spot, with an above-average 12 percent of commuters sharing a ride to work.

Economic Factors

Mesa's economy is really Phoenix's economy. Besides a Boeing plant and some biotech businesses, little industry is based in the city itself. Instead, local services predominate as job opportunities, including the Mesa Arts Center opened in 2005 and other attractions for tourists that generate many additional jobs.

The city could capitalize on its fast growth with green building, which would help boost the local market for related expertise and products in this fast-growing sector. But as of early 2006, the city had no LEED Certified buildings, and one building registered with the US Green Building Council's LEED program.

Summary/Next Steps

Now that Mesa has become a large city, city officials and citizens have an opportunity to work together to address the problems generated by rapid development: traffic congestion (#30), deteriorating air quality, and the need for better public transit and land use planning. Increasing access to local food and providing incentives for green building could be woven into improvements in transit, zoning and land use. The development of more public parks would enable people to stay local, rather than getting in their cars to enjoy the desert air outside of town.

In terms of environmental priorities, Mesa's Environmental Management Program needs to be able to address big issues such as air quality, overall development planning and environmental impacts, greenhouse gas emissions, water conservation and drinking water quality. While the city might be addressing these issues in some way, it would do well to make its efforts more obvious in order to demonstrate to residents and visitors that Mesa is planning for a sustainable future.

48

Virginia Beach, Virginia

Not Just for Tourists Anymore

Virginia Beach has 38 miles of coastline on the Chesapeake Bay and Atlantic Ocean, including 28 miles of public beaches, and actively promotes its beach-oriented lifestyle. The attraction of its geographic advantages have helped make Virginia Beach a safe, prosperous, well-educated community. The question is how well the city confronts risks related to both natural disaster and continued reliance on fossil fuels.

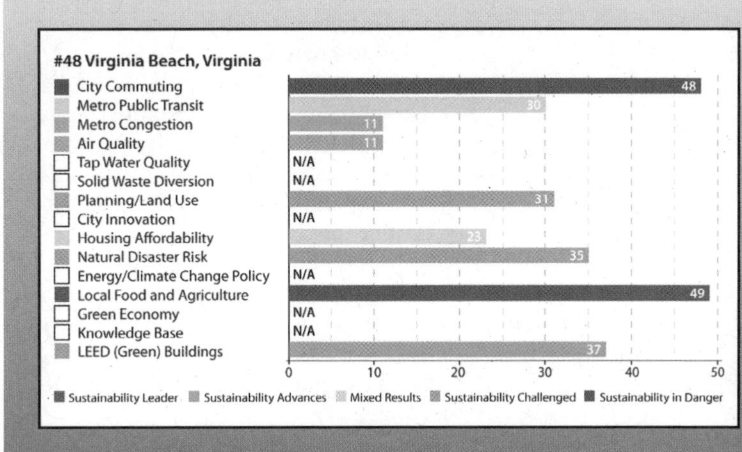

Healthy Living

Despite low overall marks, Virginia Beach citizens and visitors do enjoy decent air (#11), a fair amount of open space (#25 in percentage of park land) with 60 miles of bike trails and easy access to the coast. The city is also home to three major state and regional parks and three wildlife refuges. The quality of Virginia Beach tap water quality is unknown, as it was not available in Environmental Working Group's national database from December 2005. Farmers' markets and community gardens haven't caught on here despite the presence of 147 farms within the city.

Getting Around

One popular way to see the sights is by trolley. Apparently, however, the trolley is "just for tourists" — the city has park-and-ride lots to encourage commuting, but such efforts are almost entirely ignored by residents. In 2004, nearly 83 percent of commuters drove alone in their cars, while another 10 percent carpooled. Only 1 percent of residents walked to work and less than 1 percent took public transportation or bicycled.

Virginia Beach also operates a ferry system that is most heavily used on the weekends — residents seem to use their cars for work and use public transit for recreation. Since traffic congestion in Virginia

Beach is relatively low (#11), there seems to be little incentive for people not to drive.

Economic Factors

Virginia Beach's economy is strong overall; median incomes are higher than average for the region, and housing affordability ranks #23. As of May 2006, the city's largest employer, the Oceana Naval Air Station, remained threatened with closure by the federal government due to encroaching development. Virginia Beach continues to court defense contracts by touting its high tech defense and security resources. Retail trade, agribusiness, manufacturing and convention business are other major industries.

Virginia Beach is home to at least one solar energy company, and a variety of other renewable energy enterprises pepper its surrounding communities. In late 2005, the city announced the awarding of the first LEED certification of any building in Virginia to Hermitage Elementary School. The city's mixed-use Town Center is a positive move toward reducing reliance on cars.

Summary/Next Steps

Virginia Beach has an opportunity to capitalize on its geographic advantages to create a truly sustainable city. It has the farms to support a robust local food economy, and could benefit by tying those producers to local farmers' markets, schools and other consumers. Such a local food system would reduce the impacts of long-distance food transportation, including air pollution and costly oil dependence. The city has an opportunity to be a green economy leader in Virginia by creating incentives for additional green buildings and supporting the renewable energy enterprises in the region.

Another day at the beach. Virginia Beach's coastal location is an asset as well as a risk.

Wikipedia / GNU FDL1.2

49

Oklahoma City, Oklahoma

Planting a Few Seeds

In the early 1900s, Oklahoma City was a charming Victorian city with a trolley system, a significant commercial center, a railway hub and productive industry. The discovery of oil in 1928 was a great boon for the city, bringing an influx of rural migrants and unemployed workers during the Depression. The city continued to thrive after WWII until the 1960s, when the oil under the city dried up and property values began to decline.

As with so many other US cities, the inner core of Oklahoma City began a dramatic decline in the 1960s, which led to "white flight" to the rapidly developing suburbs in the 1970s. In response, several urban renewal projects were implemented, resulting in the demolition of old neighborhoods, the aging theater district and historical buildings like the Biltmore Hotel. When money for the renewal ran dry, vacant lots sat empty where brownstones once stood. Redeveloping these areas offers one path toward creating a more sustainable city.

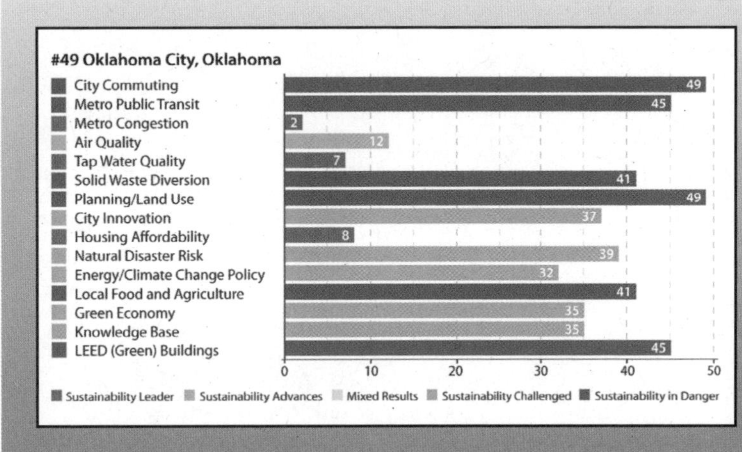

Healthy Living

Two areas where Oklahoma City shines are air quality (#12) and tap water quality (#7). Admirably, the city is highly conscious of the importance of water. Water awareness is taught in school, and the city even has a "Drinking Water Week."

Locally grown produce is scarce. There are only three farmers' markets in the city, which ranks #41 for local food and agriculture. On the bright side, the Oklahoma Food Cooperative distributes all kinds of locally grown and produced food to cities throughout Oklahoma. The organization is now helping people throughout the region start locally grown food co-ops in their own communities.

There are a limited number of city parks (#44 in park percentage of total land), but the city is implementing a new trail system that is meant to serve as a sort of bicycle freeway. Walking, running, biking and skating paths will stretch across Oklahoma City and many of its suburbs. Several walking trails around the lakes and downtown are already completed.

Getting Around

The days of trolley-based travel in Oklahoma City are long gone. Transportation money goes into highways, not public transportation, and 85 percent of the population commutes alone by car, compared to less than 1 percent who commute by public transportation and 1.5 percent who walk or bike to work. Overall, Oklahoma City ranks #49 in city commuting and #45 in metro area public transportation. There are no carpool or carshare programs in the city. In the 1990s there was some talk about light rail, but it stalled. A present plan does involve a light rail trolley, a commuter rail from downtown to the suburbs, and a metropolitan bus network.

Addressing the state of transportation in Oklahoma City, Mayor Mick Cornett lamented in *The Oklahoman* (April 18, 2006): "I think from a public transit standpoint, we are not prepared [for an energy crisis]. We have designed and created a culture in this city for the automobile. The day when the automobile is no longer an option, this city is going to have to adapt quickly to the things other cities have done for a long time."

A recent restoration has transformed downtown Oklahoma City into a popular destination.

Economic Factors

A recent restoration has transformed downtown Oklahoma City into a popular destination. The former warehouse district, Bricktown, is now a bustling entertainment district. Many other neighborhoods have also been restored, offering upscale lofts, galleries, offices and shops.

Despite this growth, none of the redevelopment has included a sustainable living component. As far as SustainLane could determine, the city has only one green (LEED certified) building, no city environmental department, no sustainability plan and no significant (greater than 1 percent) renewable energy sources as part of its overall city supply.

The city has hung its hopes on the fossil fuels energy industry, which, industry supporters have argued, will buffer the local economy against the higher energy costs being borne by citizens. To some degree they may be right: Higher oil and natural gas prices will benefit local energy companies such as Kerr-McGee, and some of that money will be respent in the state's economy. But overall money spent by people in the region on rising energy costs — most of which will go overseas — dwarfs any regional job-gain economic benefit that may result from higher energy prices.

Summary/Next Steps

Oklahoma City's air and water quality, its downtown redevelopment, and its light rail plans are strengths from which to build.

The city would benefit from better public transportation alternatives while educating the community about the importance to the economy of a strong public transit system. The expanded availability of the local food supply and support of other local businesses enabling a healthy economy would provide an economy less vulnerable to the volatility of the boom-and-bust fossil fuel industry. It might also consider creating a city environmental role, which would be an excellent way to support and track sustainable projects and policy citywide.

Fortunately, Oklahoma has many neighboring cities whose programs in coordinating sustainability and environmental offices could serve as models, including Dallas, San Antonio and Houston.

COURTESY OKC CONVENTION & VISITORS BUREAU

Myriad Botanical Gardens, a gem of biodiversity in Oklahoma City.

50

Columbus, Ohio

Time to Get Green

Smack dab in the center of Ohio on the Scioto and Olentangy rivers, Columbus is the state capital and host to Ohio State University, as well as a transit hub for rail freight and trucking. Its city center, though, has never caught on as a hub of redevelopment and revitalization — the city's energies and population have flowed ever outward on asphalted spokes.

In 2005, Mayor Michael B. Coleman launched a Columbus "Get Green" policy that targeted air quality, recycling and green building. The city has made a number of improvements around recycling, and has a huge opportunity to take action by developing sustainability programs.

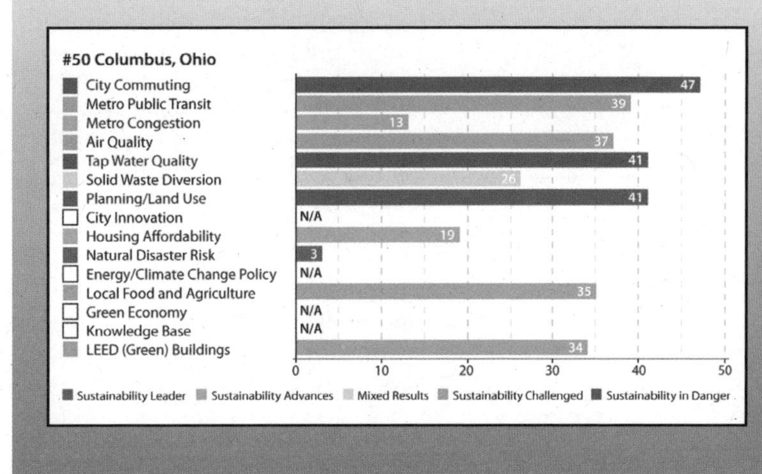

Healthy Living

The air in Columbus ranks #37, with an EPA ozone air quality violation in 2004-2005. As part of Get Green, an anti-idling measure for municipal vehicles was put into effect, but efforts to control air pollution will need to go beyond limiting idling vehicles. The roots of the city's overall low ranking in our study are the pervasiveness of vehicles, their frequent use, and the lack of an infrastructure encouraging viable alternatives.

Tap water ranks at #41 in our study, as it contains 18 contaminants, 6 of which are over the recommended limits set by the EPA.

Parks take up about 6 percent of the city's total land, which is on the lower end of an average range for a US city. The largest city park, Three Creeks, is a major hub in the Franklin County Greenways program, an interconnected system of trails along seven major streams in Central Ohio. The 13 miles of trails parallel the streams, winding through forests, fields, prairies and wetlands. Most other area parks are under the management of Metro

The Central Ohio Bicycle Advocacy Organization does just what its name suggests, including sponsoring city group rides to build community and raise awareness about cycling.

Parks, which includes 13 suburban parks splayed out around the circumference of Interstate 270, which forms the city's outer rings.

Getting Around

Without any commuter rail, light rail or metro system, Columbus commuters rely almost exclusively on their cars, which they drive alone in great numbers — more than 83 percent. Though the city has a bus system, less than 3 percent of residents use it to commute. Only about 2 percent of people in town walk or bike to work. Because the town is bisected by two diverging Interstates, non-vehicular movement is somewhat impeded.

The Central Ohio Bicycle Advocacy Organization does just what its name suggests, including sponsoring city group rides to build community and raise awareness about cycling.

Economic Factors

Columbus is a classic Midwestern city, with major industry in heavy manufacturing, printing, insurance and retail clothing company headquarters. It's also home to the headquarters of the hamburger restaurant corporations Wendy's and White Castle. Many national retailers use Columbus as a baseline for product launch testing.

In terms of a green economy, there are few indicators of such activity in Columbus. The city had four LEED buildings registered as of early 2006 (though the city in 2006 was ready to open one of the nation's largest LEED certified buildings, a former downtown department store). Renewable energy businesses, local food and a local green business directory are also lacking. Green Energy Ohio is attempting to fix that situation by promoting news, tours and legislation for renewable energy throughout the state.

Summary/Next Steps

Columbus would be best served by confronting head-on its dependency on the automobile and fossil fuel energy. The city is in danger of becoming less competitive economically as its citizens feel the pinch of higher gas prices. With no viable public transit, more and more of their hard-earned money will be spent on just getting around — reducing income for spending on restaurants, entertainment and nonessential shopping.

It makes sense for Columbus to expand its fleet of public transit buses and to examine developing other forms of public transit as well. Besides improving the city's air quality, such actions would provide insurance against energy-related economic woes.

The Lurie Garden at Millennium Park, Chicago.

Part III

Cities by Category Ranking

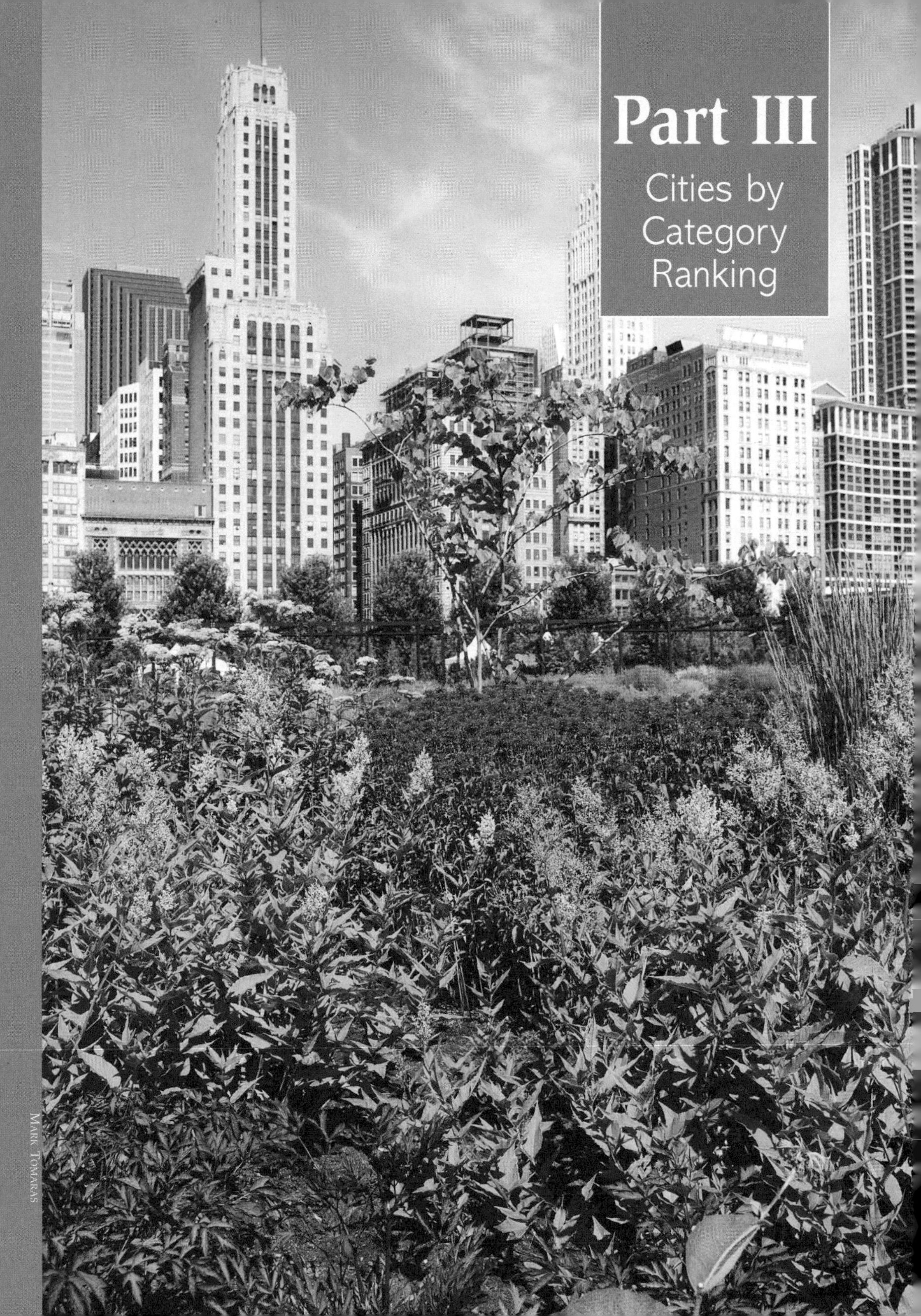

Mark Tomaras

Ken Ott

City Commuting

Data was collected from the US Bureau of the Census/American Fact Finder.

Washington, DC leads the nation in this category, with the second-highest use of public transit in the nation at more than 33 percent, the highest walk-to-work rating at more than 11 percent, and above-average bike-to-work ratings.

Following close behind are #2 New York City, the leader in public transit use with 53 percent of residents commuting on it, and #3 San Francisco, which has good all-around commute rates in public transit, biking and walking to work. Boston and Philadelphia are #4 and #5, respectively — both have excellent or good public transit ridership rates.

At the bottom end of the spectrum, some cities have less than 2 percent of citizens commuting on public transit, with less than 1 percent of citizens walking to work.

Denver, with a 5 percent commute to work rate on public transit, has plans to increase that figure fourfold or fivefold over the next decades through an ambitious transit-oriented development.

City Commuting *denotes tie

Rank	City	Rank	City
1	Washington, DC	26	Fresno, CA
2	New York, NY	27	Las Vegas, NV
3	San Francisco, CA	28	Dallas, TX
4	Boston, MA	29	Charlotte, NC
5	Philadelphia, PA	30	Colorado Springs, CO*
6	Chicago, IL	30	Jacksonville, FL*
7	Baltimore, MD	32	El Paso, TX*
8	Seattle, WA	32	Mesa, AZ*
9	Honolulu, HI	34	Austin, TX
10	Portland, OR*	35	Tulsa, OK*
10	Oakland, CA*	35	Memphis, TN*
12	Minneapolis, MN	37	Kansas City, MO
13	Miami, FL	38	San Jose, CA
14	Cleveland, OH	39	Arlington, TX
15	Milwaukee, WI	40	San Antonio, TX
16	New Orleans, LA	41	Louisville, KY
17	Los Angeles, CA	42	Omaha, NE
18	Atlanta, GA	43	Nashville, TN
19	Tucson, AZ*	44	San Diego, CA
19	Houston, TX*	45	Albuquerque, NM*
21	Detroit, MI	45	Indianapolis, IN*
22	Denver, CO	47	Columbus, OH
23	Phoenix, AZ	48	Virginia Beach, VA
24	Long Beach, CA	49	Oklahoma City, OK
25	Sacramento, CA	50	Fort Worth, TX

Source: US Bureau of Census and American FactFinder

WIKIPEDIA / GNU FDL1.2

Regional Public Transportation Ridership

Data was collected from the Texas Transportation Institute's Urban Mobility Study (Texas A&M).

Rankings were based on metro region public transit ridership miles and square miles per region.

Regional Public Transportation Ridership — *denotes tie

Rank	City	Rank	City
1	New York, NY	26	Milwaukee, WI
2	Chicago, IL	27	Austin, TX
3	Boston, MA	28	Honolulu, HI
4	Oakland, CA*	29	San Antonio, TX
4	San Francisco, CA*	30	Virginia Beach, VA
6	Washington, DC	31	New Orleans, LA
7	Philadelphia, PA	32	Jacksonville, FL
8	Long Beach, CA*	33	Sacramento, CA
8	Los Angeles, CA*	34	Charlotte, NC
10	Atlanta, GA	35	San Jose, CA
11	Seattle, WA	36	Kansas City, MO
12	Houston, TX	37	Memphis, TN
13	Miami, FL	38	Las Vegas, NV
14	Baltimore, MD	39	Columbus, OH
15	Arlington, TX	40	Indianapolis, IN*
15	Dallas, TX	40	Tucson, AZ*
15	Fort Worth, TX	42	El Paso, TX*
18	Minneapolis, MN	42	Nashville, TN*
19	Denver, CO	44	Louisville, KY
20	Portland, OR	45	Oklahoma City, OK
21	Cleveland, OH	46	Fresno, CA
22	San Diego, CA	47	Albuquerque, NM
23	Detroit, MI	48	Colorado Springs, CO*
24	Mesa, AZ*	48	Tulsa, OK*
24	Phoenix, AZ*	50	Omaha, NE

Source: Texas Transportation Institute Urban Mobility Study

PARK
DEPOT
7044
CA 49819
GREEN has seats for 48 passengers.
7044

Ken Ott

Metro Street and Freeway Congestion

Data was collected from the Texas Transportation Institute's Urban Mobility Study (Texas A&M), which examined average time spent waiting in traffic.

Cleveland is the least congested of the 50 largest US cities. Following close behind are #2 Tulsa and Oklahoma City (tied), #4 Fresno, and #5 Kansas City.

Metro Street and Freeway Congestion *denotes tie

Rank	City	Rank	City
1	Cleveland, OH	26	Minneapolis, MN*
2	Tulsa, OK*	26	Charlotte, NC*
2	Oklahoma City, OK*	28	Seattle, WA
4	Fresno, CA	29	New York, NY
5	Kansas City, MO	30	Phoenix, AZ*
6	El Paso, TX*	30	Mesa, AZ*
6	New Orleans, LA*	32	Baltimore, MD
8	Honolulu, HI	33	Boston, MA
9	Milwaukee, WI*	34	Austin, TX
9	Omaha, NE*	35	Miami, FL
11	Virginia Beach, VA	36	Denver, CO
12	Colorado Springs, CO	37	San Diego, CA
13	Columbus, OH	38	Detroit, MI
14	Las Vegas, NV	39	Chicago, IL
15	San Antonio, TX*	40	San Jose, CA
15	Memphis, TN*	41	Arlington, TX*
17	Jacksonville, FL	41	Dallas, TX*
18	Albuquerque, NM	41	Fort Worth, TX*
19	Tucson, AZ	44	Houston, TX
20	Nashville, TN	45	Atlanta, GA
21	Philadelphia, PA*	46	Washington, DC
21	Indianapolis, IN*	47	Oakland, CA*
23	Portland, OR	47	San Francisco, CA*
24	Sacramento, CA	49	Long Beach, CA*
25	Louisville, KY	49	Los Angeles, CA*

Source: Texas Transportation Institute Urban Mobility Study

Wikipedia / GNU FDL1.2

Air Quality

Air Quality was determined by EPA data on average Air Quality Indexes, combined with EPA data on Non-Attainment areas for the Clean Air Act.

Honolulu had the cleanest average air among the 50 largest US cities studied. Following in rank for best air quality are #2 Portland, Oregon; #3 San Francisco; #4 Oakland; and #5 Minneapolis.

Air quality is partially determined by natural forces including geography, weather and wind patterns, so the highest-ranking cities in some cases have their physical location to thank.

But by no means does a city's poor air quality mean that it can't take steps to markedly improve conditions. Number-two city Portland, for instance, had some of the nation's worst air pollution in the 1960s and early 1970s, before it worked with industry and developed urban planning measures to reduce smog-producing sprawl.

Now Portland ranks as one of the most desirable cities, attracting young professionals — with the city's clean air quality being considered a major benefit of the city's environment.

Air Quality *denotes tie

Rank	City	Rank	City
1	Honolulu, HI	22	Memphis, TN*
2	Portland, OR	22	Fort Worth, TX*
3	San Francisco, CA	28	Milwaukee, WI
4	Oakland, CA	29	Cleveland, OH
5	Minneapolis, MN	30	Philadelphia, PA
6	New Orleans, LA	31	Lousiville, KY
7	Seattle, WA*	32	Washington, DC*
7	Austin, TX*	32	Las Vegas, NV*
7	San Jose, CA*	32	El Paso, TX*
7	Miami, FL*	32	Nashville, TN*
11	Virginia Beach, VA	36	Baltimore, MD
12	Colorado Springs, CO*	37	Charlotte, NC*
12	Oklahoma City, OK*	37	Columbus, OH*
12	Denver, CO*	39	Atlanta, GA
12	San Antonio, TX*	40	Houston, TX
12	Tucson, AZ*	41	Indianapolis, IN
12	Omaha, NE*	42	New York, NY
12	Tulsa, OK*	43	Sacramento, CA*
12	Kansas City, MO*	43	Fresno, CA*
12	Jacksonville, FL*	43	Chicago, IL*
21	San Diego, CA	43	Phoenix, AZ*
22	Boston, MA*	43	Mesa, AZ*
22	Albuquerque, NM*	48	Detroit, MI
22	Dallas, TX*	49	Los Angeles, CA*
22	Arlington, TX*	49	Long Beach, CA*

Source: US Environmental Protection Agency

Chris73 / Wikimedia / CreativeCommons 2.5

Tap Water Quality

Data was analyzed from the Environmental Working Group's December 2005 database of city tap water quality, which was collected from the US Environmental Protection Agency.

The highest-ranking tap water in the study was in Kansas City, which had no recorded pollutants when tested.

Following in rank for best tap water quality are #2 Portland; #3 Louisville; #4 San Francisco; #5 Memphis; #6 San Antonio; #7 Oklahoma City; #8 Fort Worth; #9 Jacksonville; and #10 Arlington.

Data was unavailable for Honolulu, New Orleans, New York, and Virginia Beach.

Tap Water Quality *denotes tie

Rank	City	Rank	City
1	Kansas City, MO	26	Indianapolis, IN
2	Portland, OR	27	Charlotte, NC
3	Louisville, KY	28	Colorado Springs, CO
4	San Francisco, CA	29	Chicago, IL
5	Memphis, TN	30	Houston, TX
6	San Antonio, TX	31	Cleveland, OH
7	Oklahoma City, OK	32	Milwaukee, WI
8	Fort Worth, TX	33	Omaha, NE
9	Jacksonville, FL	34	Mesa, AZ
10	Arlington, TX	35	Phoenix, AZ
11	Dallas, TX	36	Detroit, MI
12	San Jose, CA	37	Oakland, CA
13	Baltimore, MD	38	Minneapolis, MI
14	El Paso, TX	39	Atlanta, GA
15	Sacramento, CA	40	Boston, MA
16	Seattle, WA	41	Columbus, OH
17	Philadelphia, PA	42	Las Vegas, NV
18	Denver, CO	43	Nashville, TN
19	Austin, TX	44	San Diego, CA
20	Long Beach, CA	45	Washington, DC
21	Albuquerque, NM	46	Los Angeles, CA
22	Miami, FL	N/A	Honolulu, HI
23	Tucson, AZ	N/A	New Orleans, LA
24	Fresno, CA	N/A	New York, NY
25	Tulsa, OK	N/A	Virginia Beach, VA

Source: Environmental Working Group and US Environmental Protection Agency

Kai-Hua Cheng

Kai-Hua Cheng

Solid Waste Diversion

Tied for #1 are a number of cities in California, which mandates a waste diversion minimum for cities, and tracks waste diversion rates for all the cities in the state as part of this state program. San Francisco, San Jose, Long Beach, and Los Angeles all divert more than 60 percent of their total waste from city landfills through recycling, green waste and composting programs.

Solid Waste Diversion — *denotes tie

Rank	City	Rank	City
1	Long Beach, CA*	26	Albuquerque, NM*
1	Los Angeles, CA*	26	Arlington, TX*
1	San Francisco, CA*	26	Boston, MA*
1	San Jose, CA*	26	Charlotte, NC*
5	Oakland, CA*	26	Columbus, OH*
5	Portland, OR*	26	Detroit, MI*
5	Sacramento, CA*	26	Houston, TX*
5	San Diego, CA*	26	Indianapolis, IN*
9	Chicago, IL*	26	Las Vegas, NV*
9	Louisville, KY*	26	Mesa, AZ*
9	Nashville, TN*	26	Miami, FL*
9	New York, NY*	26	New Orleans, LA*
9	Seattle, WA*	26	Phoenix, AZ*
14	Jacksonville, FL	26	Tulsa, OK*
15	Baltimore, MD*	26	Washington, DC
15	Fresno, CA*	41	Cleveland, OH*
15	Honolulu, HI*	41	Colorado Springs, CO*
15	Kansas City, MO*	41	Dallas, TX*
15	Minneapolis, MN*	41	Denver, CO*
20	Atlanta, GA*	41	El Paso, TX*
20	Austin, TX*	41	Oklahoma City, OK*
20	Fort Worth, TX*	41	Philadelphia, PA*
20	Memphis, TN*	41	Tucson, AZ*
20	San Antonio, TX*	N/A	Omaha, NE
25	Milwaukee, WI	N/A	Virginia Beach, VA

Source: SustainLane

Washington, DC Convention and Tourism Corporation

City of Santa Monica

Planning and Land Use

Data analyzed included park percentage per total city land from the Trust for Public Land as well as sprawl ranking, which was developed by the Smart Growth America 2002 study of US cities.

San Francisco ranks #1 overall in planning, with about 20 percent of its land devoted to parks (#1 in that subcategory), combined with a sprawl rating that is second best out of the nation's top 50 cities. New York, Boston, Portland, Albuquerque, El Paso and Omaha (tied), and Philadelphia follow.

Planning and Land Use

*denotes tie

Rank	City	Rank	City
1	San Francisco, CA	25	Long Beach, CA*
2	New York, NY	25	Nashville, TN*
3	Boston, MA	28	New Orleans, LA
4	Portland, OR	29	Minneapolis, MN
5	Albuquerque, NM	30	San Antonio, TX
6	El Paso, TX*	31	Sacramento, CA*
6	Omaha, NE*	31	Virginia Beach, VA*
8	Philadelphia, PA	33	Jacksonville, FL
9	Baltimore, MD*	34	Tulsa, OK*
9	Phoenix, AZ*	34	Dallas, TX*
11	Austin, TX*	36	Mesa, AZ
11	San Diego, CA*	37	Kansas City, MO
13	Milwaukee, WI	38	San Jose, CA
14	Colorado Springs, CO	39	Fresno, CA*
15	Chicago, IL*	39	Memphis, TN*
15	Louisville, KY*	41	Columbus, OH
17	Denver, CO	42	Tucson, AZ
18	Charlotte, NC	43	Detroit, MI
19	Seattle, WA	44	Houston, TX
20	Washington, DC	45	Arlington, TX
21	Los Angeles, CA	46	Cleveland, OH
22	Honolulu, HI	47	Indianapolis, IN
23	Oakland, CA	48	Fort Worth, TX
24	Miami, FL	49	Oklahoma City, OK
25	Las Vegas, NV*	50	Atlanta, GA

Source: Trust for Public Land and SustainLane

City of Santa Monica

City Innovation

For city innovation, SustainLane analyzed the following categories using primary research:

- City commercial green building incentives
- Environmentally preferable purchasing programs
- City residential green building incentives
- Carpooling coordination
- Carsharing programs (public or private)
- One other significant city innovation not accounted for in the other five areas was credited to some cities as a bonus credit.

Portland, Sacramento and Seattle tied at #1, demonstrating programs in all six subcategories. Tied at #4 are Chicago, New York and Tucson. The 37 cities that responded to the survey are included in this list.

City Innovation *denotes tie

Rank	City	Rank	City
1	Portland, OR*	26	Indianapolis, IN
1	Sacramento, CA*	27	Dallas, TX
1	Seattle, WA*	28	Charlotte, NC*
4	Chicago, IL*	28	Detroit, MI*
4	New York, NY*	28	Kansas City, MO*
4	Tucson, AZ*	28	Long Beach, CA*
7	Denver, CO*	28	Milwaukee, WI*
7	Fresno, CA*	28	Philadelphia, PA*
7	Los Angeles, CA*	28	San Antonio, TX*
7	Minneapolis, MN*	35	Honolulu, HI*
11	Albuquerque, NM*	35	New Orleans, LA*
11	Las Vegas, NV*	37	Oklahoma City, OK
11	Louisville, KY*	N/A	Austin, TX
11	Oakland, CA*	N/A	Cleveland, OH
11	Phoenix, AZ*	N/A	Miami, FL
11	San Diego, CA*	N/A	El Paso, TX
11	San Francisco, CA*	N/A	Jacksonville, FL
11	Washington, DC*	N/A	Omaha, NE
19	Arlington, TX*	N/A	Atlanta, GA
19	Baltimore, MD*	N/A	Nashville, TN
19	Boston, MA*	N/A	Memphis, TN
19	Colorado Springs, CO*	N/A	Fort Worth, TX
19	Houston, TX*	N/A	Mesa, AZ
19	San Jose, CA*	N/A	Virginia Beach, VA
19	Tulsa, OK*	N/A	Columbus, OH

Source: SustainLane

Housing Affordability

SustainLane used data from the US Bureau of the Census on average housing prices and average income levels to determine city housing affordability.

Coming in at #1 for housing affordability when surveyed, San Antonio had an average home price of $88,400, an average annual income of $36,500, and a living wage ordinance. Following close behind were Baltimore; El Paso; Fort Worth; and Arlington, Texas.

Housing Affordability *denotes tie

Rank	City	Rank	City
1	San Antonio, TX	26	Phoenix, AZ
2	Baltimore, MD	27	Milwaukee, WI
3	El Paso, TX	28	Austin, TX
4	Fort Worth, TX	29	Colorado Springs, CO
5	Arlington, TX	30	New Orleans, LA
6	Tulsa, OK	31	Minneapolis, MI
7	Cleveland, OH*	32	Portland, OR
7	Oklahoma City, OK*	33	Las Vegas, NV
9	Memphis, TN	34	Fresno, CA
10	Detroit, MI	35	Denver, CO
11	Indianapolis, IN	36	Chicago, IL
12	Philadelphia, PA	37	Washington, DC*
13	Houston, TX	37	Atlanta, GA*
14	Omaha, NE	39	Sacramento, CA
15	Kansas City, OK	40	Seattle, WA
16	Jacksonville, FL	41	San Jose, CA
17	Dallas, TX	42	Boston, MA
18	Louisville, KY	43	Miami, FL
19	Columbus, OH	44	Oakland, CA
20	Nashville, TN	45	Honolulu, HI
21	Charlotte, NC	46	New York, NY
22	Tucson, AZ	47	San Diego, CA
23	Virginia Beach, VA	48	Los Angeles, CA
24	Mesa, AZ	49	San Francisco, CA
25	Albuquerque, NM	50	Long Beach, CA

Source: US Bureau of Census

Natural Disaster Risk

SustainLane examined the 50 largest US cities based on natural disaster risk. This ranking was devised with SustainLane primary research as well as with information from Risk Management Solutions (see chart for complete ranking of cities from safest to most at risk). We looked at hurricanes, major flooding, catastrophic hail, tornado super-outbreaks and earthquakes, taking into consideration potential frequency of disasters as well as the extent of damage.

Natural disasters can have significant environmental and economic impacts on cities, as can be evidenced by the destruction Katrina caused in New Orleans. SustainLane did not analyze drought in this category, as this natural phenomenon may be mitigated by water importation and conservation. Urban wildfires were also not analyzed as part of this study, as wildfire damage in modern cities typically impacts only limited areas — the Oakland, California Firestorm of 1991 is one tragic exception. The cities that follow were ranked by risk of natural disasters that could change the landscape of a city in a short period of time, impacting most city structures, water and energy supplies, in addition to the catastrophic loss of life.

Natural Disaster Risk *denotes tie

Rank	City	Rank	City
1	Miami, FL	26	Indianapolis, IN
2	New Orleans, LA	27	Fort Worth, TX*
3	Oakland, CA	27	Dallas, TX*
4	San Francisco, CA	27	Arlington, TX*
5	Honolulu, HI	30	Kansas City, MO
6	San Jose, CA	31	Austin, TX
7	Los Angeles, CA*	32	Omaha, NE
7	Houston, TX*	33	Atlanta, GA
9	Long Beach, CA	34	Nashville, TN
10	Tulsa, OK*	35	San Antonio, TX
10	Oklahoma City, OK*	36	Las Vegas, NV
10	Columbus, OH*	37	Albuquerque, NM
13	Sacramento, CA	38	Denver, CO
14	Virginia Beach, VA*	39	Chicago, IL
14	Seattle, WA*	40	Philadelphia, PA*
14	Memphis, TN*	40	Minneapolis, MN*
17	New York, NY*	40	Fresno, CA*
17	Jacksonville, FL*	40	Detroit, MI*
17	Boston, MA*	44	Colorado Springs, CO
20	San Diego, CA	45	Tucson, AZ*
21	Portland, OR	45	Phoenix, AZ*
22	Charlotte, NC	45	El Paso, TX*
23	Baltimore, MD	45	Cleveland, OH*
24	Washington, DC	49	Milwaukee, WI*
25	Louisville, KY	49	Mesa, AZ*

Source: Risk Management Solutions and SustainLane

Cities at Greatest Risk

Based on these criteria, the cities with the greatest natural disaster risk are Miami (#50), which is sited on a peninsula between two prolific hurricane zones; New Orleans (#49); Oakland (#48), which straddles the Hayward Earthquake Fault; San Francisco (#47), on the San Andreas Fault and at risk for tsunamis; Honolulu (#46), subject to hurricanes, storm surge flooding and tsunamis; and San Jose (#45), which is also near the San Andreas Earthquake Fault.

Cities at Least Risk

Some US cities are much less likely to be impacted by such catastrophic natural disasters. Leading the pack for safe cities when considering such scenarios are Mesa, (#1) and Milwaukee (#1), both of which are least likely to face hurricanes, earthquakes, catastrophic hail and tornado super-outbreaks, as they lack geographic, geologic and atmospheric conditions needed to create these disasters. Catastrophic flooding is also not as likely. Other major US cities ranking high for safety from natural disaster risk include Cleveland, El Paso, Phoenix and Tucson (all ranked #3).

KAI-HUA CHENG

Energy and Climate Change Policy

SustainLane primary research in this category analyzed:

- City greenhouse gas tracking and carbon emission inventories
- Carbon emission reduction goals
- Overall renewable energy use
- Percentage for each city's alternative fueled vehicles as part of the total vehicle fleet was credited to cities with such fleets of greater than 12 percent of total fleet.

Greenhouse gas emissions are a major contributor to global climate change, and renewable energy use and alternative-fuel use mitigate carbon and air pollution production while driving local or regional job growth and economic competitiveness.

Coming in at #1 for energy and climate change policy as defined by the above criteria are three cities that scored 4/4: Portland; San Francisco; and Seattle. Los Angeles ranks #4.

Energy and Climate Change Policy *denotes tie

Rank	City	Rank	City
1	Portland, OR*	24	Indianapolis, IN*
1	San Francisco, CA*	24	Las Vegas, NV*
1	Seattle, WA*	24	Louisville, KY*
4	Los Angeles, CA	24	Phoenix, AZ*
5	Albuquerque, NM*	24	San Jose, CA*
5	Chicago, IL*	31	Milwaukee, WI
5	New York, NY*	32	Arlington, TX*
5	Philadelphia, PA*	32	Baltimore, MD*
5	San Diego, CA*	32	Charlotte, NC*
10	Denver, CO*	32	Oklahoma City, OK*
10	Minneapolis, MN*	32	Tulsa, OK*
12	Oakland, CA*	N/A	Atlanta, GA
12	Sacramento, CA*	N/A	Austin, TX
12	San Antonio, TX*	N/A	Cleveland, OH
15	Dallas, TX*	N/A	Columbus, OH
15	New Orleans, LA*	N/A	Detroit, MI
17	Boston, MA*	N/A	El Paso, TX
17	Colorado Springs, CO*	N/A	Fort Worth, TX
17	Fresno, CA*	N/A	Jacksonville, FL
17	Kansas City, MO*	N/A	Memphis, TN
17	Long Beach, CA*	N/A	Mesa, AZ
17	Washington, DC*	N/A	Miami, FL
23	Tucscon, AZ	N/A	Nashville, TN
24	Honolulu, HI*	N/A	Omaha, NE
24	Houston, TX*	N/A	Virginia Beach, VA

Source: Sustain Lane

Kai-Hua Cheng

Kai-Hua Cheng

Local Food and Agriculture

Local food and agriculture help communities become more self-sufficient and less reliant on food transported great distances with fossil fuels. Local food is also fresher, usually has more nutrients and requires less packaging and refrigeration than food that must be shipped long distances. Local food purchases also recirculate money back into the regional economy, as farmers' market income typically gets respent in-state.

SustainLane used data from the US Department of Agriculture for farmers' markets and conducted primary research on farmers' markets and community gardens.

The leader in local food and agriculture is Boston, which has a large number of farmers' markets and community gardens per capita, and is supported by strong local food education and distribution programs. Minneapolis, at #2, also has high number of both community gardens and farmers' markets per capita. At #3, Philadelphia draws upon a healthy network of in-state farmers, with an active community gardening program sponsored by the state horticultural society. Washington, DC (#4) has strong links to its regional agricultural territory and the

Local Food and Agriculture *denotes tie

Rank	City	Rank	City
1	Boston, MA	26	Las Vegas, NV
2	Minneapolis, MN	27	Cleveland, OH
3	Philadelphia, PA	28	Charlotte, NC
4	Washington, DC	29	Omaha, NE
5	Portland, OR*	30	El Paso, TX
5	Seattle, WA*	31	Indianapolis, IN
7	Austin, TX	32	San Diego, CA
8	Honolulu, HI	33	New Orleans, LA
9	Oakland, CA	34	Tulsa, OK
10	Denver, CO	35	Columbus, OH
11	Baltimore, MD	36	Los Angeles, CA
12	San Francisco, CA	37	Mesa, AZ
13	Milwaukee, WI	38	Detroit, MI
14	Sacramento, CA	39	Atlanta, GA
15	Tucson, AZ	40	Phoenix, AZ
16	Chicago, IL	41	Oklahoma City, OK
17	New York, NY	42	Jacksonville, FL
18	San Antonio, TX	43	Louisville, KY
19	Albuquerque, NM	44	Houston, TX
20	San Jose, CA	45	Miami, FL
21	Colorado Springs, CO	46	Fort Worth, TX
22	Nashville, TN	47	Memphis, TN
23	Long Beach, CA	48	Dallas, TX
24	Kansas City, MO	49	Virginia Beach, VA
25	Fresno, CA	50	Arlington, TX

Source: US Department of Agriculture and SustainLane

second-highest rate of farmers' markets per capita. Tied at #5 are Portland and Seattle, both of which have high rates of farmers' markets per capita and significant community garden programs.

City of Santa Monica

Green Economy

Categories of analysis were based on SustainLane primary research except where noted.

- Green, or LEED (Leadership in Energy and Environmental Design) buildings per capita, which was based on data from the US Green Building Council
- Farmers' markets per capita data from US Department of Agriculture and primary research
- Presence of a city or public-private incubator for clean technology industries, including renewable energy, advanced transportation, advanced water treatment, alternative fuels, green building and energy efficiency
- Presence within the city of a green business directory, either public or private.

Green Economy does not include environmental services such as hazardous waste cleanup services.

Many elements of the Green Economy have value-added benefits for a city's local economy while reducing stress on local resources and the local ecosystem. Green

Green Economy *denotes tie

Rank	City	Rank	City
1	Portland, OR	26	Las Vegas, NV*
2	Sacramento, CA*	26	Tulsa, OK*
2	Seattle, WA*	28	Long Beach, CA
4	Philadelphia, PA	29	New Orleans, LA
5	San Francisco, CA	30	Fresno, CA
6	Denver, CO	31	Charlotte, NC
7	Oakland, CA	32	Arlington, TX
8	Baltimore, MD	33	Indianapolis, IN
9	Chicago, IL	34	San Antonio, TX
10	Milwaukee, WI	35	Detroit, MI*
11	Washington, DC	35	Oklahoma City, OK
12	Boston, MA*	37	Louisville, KY
12	Minneapolis, MN	N/A	Atlanta, GA
12	San Diego, CA*	N/A	Austin, TX
15	Honolulu, HI	N/A	Cleveland, OH
16	San Jose, CA	N/A	Columbus, OH
17	Phoenix, AZ	N/A	El Paso, TX
18	New York, NY	N/A	Fort Worth, TX
19	Albuquerque, NM	N/A	Jacksonville, FL
20	Dallas, TX*	N/A	Memphis, TN
20	Kansas City, MO*	N/A	Mesa, AZ
20	Los Angeles, CA*	N/A	Miami, FL
20	Tucson, AZ*	N/A	Nashville, TN
24	Houston, TX	N/A	Omaha, NE
25	Colorado Springs, CO	N/A	Virginia Beach, VA

Source: SustainLane

building, for example, saves businesses and residents money in operating costs while reducing environmental impacts during manufacture, use and disposal.

On top of the Green Economy category is Portland, which has a high rate of farmers' markets and green buildings per capita and numerous local green business directories. The city was not credited with having a business incubator, though it may soon be involved in a consortium with wind-energy and other clean tech businesses. Seattle and Sacramento tied at #2, with slighter fewer farmers' markets and green buildings per capita. Philadelphia ranked #4, with a clean tech incubator for electric vehicles and green building technologies. San Francisco was #5.

KAI-HUA CHENG/ SUSTAINLANE.COM

Knowledge Base and Communications

As part of this category, four areas were analyzed based on primary research conducted by SustainLane:

- Whether the city has an overall plan for sustainability
- Whether it has a sustainability or environmental department that manages and tracks sustainability efforts across the city
- Whether the city is working in collaboration with a major federal research laboratory or research university
- Whether the city is working with a non-governmental organization across the city on sustainability projects, programs or metrics — rather than just working with a single neighborhood.

Many cities tied at #1, with a perfect 4/4 across the above subcategories: Portland, San Francisco, Seattle, Chicago, Oakland, Denver, San Diego, Phoenix, Dallas and Charlotte.

Knowledge Base and Communications *denotes tie

Rank	City	Rank	City
1	Portland, OR*	26	Las Vegas, NV
1	Seattle, WA*	27	Baltimore, MD*
1	Chicago, IL*	27	Washington, DC*
1	Denver, CO*	29	Arlington, TX*
1	Oakland, CA*	29	Colorado Springs, CO*
1	Phoenix, AZ*	29	Houston, TX*
1	San Diego, CA*	29	Tulsa, OK*
1	San Francisco, CA*	29	Detroit, MI*
1	Dallas, TX*	29	New Orleans, LA*
1	Charlotte, NC*	35	Long Beach, CA*
11	Sacramento, CA*	35	Honolulu, HI*
11	New York, NY*	35	Oklahoma City, OK*
11	Tucson, AZ*	N/A	Atlanta, GA
11	Minneapolis, MN*	N/A	Austin, TX
15	Albuquerque, NM*	N/A	Cleveland, OH
15	Louisville, KY	N/A	Columbus, OH
17	Fresno, CA*	N/A	El Paso, TX
17	Los Angeles, CA*	N/A	Fort Worth, TX
17	Boston, MA*	N/A	Jacksonville, FL
17	San Jose, CA*	N/A	Memphis, TN
17	Indianapolis, IN*	N/A	Mesa, AZ
17	Kansas City, MO*	N/A	Miami, FL
17	Milwaukee, WI*	N/A	Nashville, TN
17	Philadelphia, PA*	N/A	Omaha, NE
17	San Antonio, TX*	N/A	Virginia Beach, VA

Source: Sustain Lane

City of Santa Monica

Green (LEED) Building

This category was based on data from the United States Green Building Council's Leadership in Energy and Environmental Design (LEED) rating system.

Credit was awarded for LEED Certified buildings, with further points awarded for buildings designated in three ascending LEED tiers: Silver, Gold and Platinum. Less credit was given for LEED Registered buildings, which are typically in the planning or development phase, before receiving certification. The resulting total was then normalized on a per capita basis, using the adjusted number of LEED buildings per 100,000 people.

The #1 city based on the above analysis was Atlanta. Atlanta's 45 registered and 12 certified LEED buildings topped #2 Portland, which had 54 registered and 16 certified, but a larger population than Atlanta. In the #3 position was Seattle, with 43 registered and 14 certified LEED buildings. At #4, Washington, DC had 28 registered and 8 certified buildings, and Sacramento was #5 with 10 registered and 8 certified.

Green (LEED) Building — *denotes tie

Rank	City	Rank	City
1	Atlanta, GA	26	Tucson, AZ
2	Portland, OR	27	Nashville, TN
3	Seattle, WA	28	Phoenix, AZ
4	Washington, DC	29	Houston, TX
5	Sacramento, CA	30	Los Angeles, CA
6	San Francisco, CA	31	Charlotte, NC
7	Boston, MA	32	Detroit, MI
8	Austin, TX	33	Miami, FL
9	Philadelphia, PA	34	Columbus, OH
10	Honolulu, HI	35	Minneapolis, MI
11	Las Vegas, NV	36	El Paso, TX
12	San Diego, CA	37	Virginia Beach, VA
13	Cleveland, OH	38	Fresno, CA
14	Denver, CO	39	New York, NY
15	Chicago, IL	40	Tulsa, OK
16	Kansas City, MO	41	Jacksonville, FL
17	Oakland, CA	42	Indianapolis, IN
18	San Jose, CA	43	Mesa, AZ
19	Dallas, TX	44	New Orleans, LA
20	Baltimore, MD	45	Oklahoma City, OK
21	Milwaukee, WI	46	Fort Worth, TX
22	Omaha, NE	47	San Antonio, TX
23	Long Beach, CA	48	Louisville, KY*
24	Albuquerque, NM	48	Arlington, TX*
25	Colorado Springs, CO	48	Memphis, TN*

Source: US Green Building Council

Index

D

S

T

U

V

About the author

Warren Karlenzig, Chief Strategy Officer of SustainLane, directs the SustainLane US City Rankings, a peer-reviewed sustainability benchmarking of the largest 50 U.S. cities. The Washington Post said of the rankings: "Surveys such as SustainLane's 'go a long way in terms of helping the nation understand what constitutes a better and more sustainable urban environment.' " Karlenzig has been editor in chief of Knowledge Management magazine and sustainability consultant for the federal government (US EPA, White House Office of Science and Technology) and the state of California. He is also author of A Blueprint for Greening Affordable Housing (Global Green USA) and has appeared on CNN, CNBC, The Weather Channel's "Climate Code" and in The New York Times and The Wall Street Journal. His blog is www.greenacity.com.

SustainLane

SustainLane is an internet media company dedicated to bringing green to the mainstream through three key offerings. SustainLane Government (www.SustainLane.us) provides best practices in sustainability for a network of North American state and local government officials. SustainLane.com features a directory and reviews of green products and services, and The Unsustainables is SustainLane's animated series.